THE ANCIENT
EGYPTIAN WORLD

RONALD MELLOR &
AMANDA H. PODANY
GENERAL EDITORS

THE ANCIENT
EGYPTIAN WORLD

Eric H. Cline & Jill Rubalcaba

OXFORD
UNIVERSITY PRESS

To our families

OXFORD
UNIVERSITY PRESS

Oxford University Press, Inc., publishes works
that further Oxford University's objective of excellence
in research, scholarship, and education.

Oxford   New York
Auckland   Cape Town   Dar es Salaam   Hong Kong   Karachi
Kuala Lumpur   Madrid   Melbourne   Mexico City   Nairobi
New Delhi   Shanghai   Taipei   Toronto

With offices in
Argentina   Austria   Brazil   Chile   Czech Republic   France   Greece
Guatemala   Hungary   Italy   Japan Poland   Portugal   Singapore
South Korea   Switzerland   Thailand   Turkey   Ukraine   Vietnam

Published by Oxford University Press, Inc.
198 Madison Avenue, New York, New York 10016
www.oup.com

Library of Congress Cataloging-in-Publication Data

Cline, Eric H.
The ancient Egyptian world / Eric Cline and Jill Rubalcaba.
p. cm. — (The world in ancient times)
Includes bibliographical references and index.
ISBN-13: 978-0-19-517391-8 — 978-0-19-522244-9 (Calif. ed.) — 978-0-19-522242-5 (9-vol. set)
ISBN-10: 0-19-517391-0 — 0-19-522244-X (Calif. ed.) — 0-19-522242-3 (9-vol. set)

1. Egypt—Civilization—To 332 B.C. 2. Egypt—Civilization—
332 B.C.-638 A.D. I. Rubalcaba, Jill. II. Title. III. Series.
DT61.C54 2005
932—dc22
2004017720

9 8 7 6 5 4 3 2 1

Printed in the United States on acid-free paper.

On the cover: An elaborately bandaged mummy of a calf, from Thebes.
Frontispiece: Scribes measure and record the harvest in a painting on a tomb wall.

**RONALD MELLOR &
AMANDA H. PODANY**

GENERAL EDITORS

DIANE L. BROOKS, ED. D.

EDUCATION CONSULTANT

The Early Human World
Peter Robertshaw & Jill Rubalcaba

The Ancient Near Eastern World
Amanda H. Podany & Marni McGee

The Ancient Egyptian World
Eric H. Cline & Jill Rubalcaba

The Ancient South Asian World
Jonathan Mark Kenoyer & Kimberley Heuston

The Ancient Chinese World
Terry Kleeman & Tracy Barrett

The Ancient Greek World
Jennifer T. Roberts & Tracy Barrett

The Ancient Roman World
Ronald Mellor & Marni McGee

The Ancient American World
William Fash & Mary E. Lyons

**The World in Ancient Times:
Primary Sources and Reference Volume**
Ronald Mellor & Amanda H. Podany

CONTENTS

A 🔳 *marks each chapter's primary sources—ancient writings and artifacts that "speak" to us from the past.*

CAST OF CHARACTERS

Because The World in Ancient Times *covers many cultures, we use the abbreviations* BCE *for "Before the Common Era" and* CE *for "Common Era." The traditional equivalents are* BC *for "Before Christ" and* AD *for "Anno Domini," Latin for "In the Year of Our Lord," referring to the birth of Jesus Christ.*

Achthoes (ahk-THO-ees), about 2160–2040 BCE • King of Egypt who ruled during the First Intermediate Period

Aha (ah-HAH), about 3050 BCE • King of Egypt; first king of Dynasty 1; ruled immediately after Narmer unified the two halves of the country

Ahhotep (ah-HOE-tep) **I**, about 1600 BCE • Queen of Egypt; mother of Ahmose I and Kamose, Egyptian kings who expelled the foreign Hyksos from Egypt

Ahmose (AHK-moz), about 1570 BCE • Egyptian soldier who fought against the foreign Hyksos; an inscription in his tomb records his life and accomplishments

Alexander the Great, 356–323 BCE • King of Macedon (336–323 BCE); conquered Egypt and parts of Asia

Amenemhet (ah-MEN-em-het) **I**, 1991–1962 BCE • King of Egypt; first ruler during Dynasty 12

Amenhotep (ah-men-HOE-tep) **III**, 1386–1349 BCE • King of Egypt; ruled during Dynasty 18; in contact with many foreign countries, including Greece

Amenhotep (ah-men-HOE-tep) **IV** or **Akhenaten** (ahk-ken-NAH-ton), 1350–1334 BCE • Heretic king of Egypt; replaced the gods of Egypt with the worship of a single god, Aten (the Sun Disk)

Ankhtyfy (AHNK-tee-fee), about 2100 BCE • Egyptian governor and warlord during the First Intermediate Period

Cleopatra VII, 69–30 BCE • Queen of Egypt (51–30 BCE); last of the Macedonian dynasty

Diodorus (die-uh-DOR-us) **Siculus** (SICK-u-lus), 1st century BCE • Greek historian; wrote 40 books of world history

Djoser (ZO-zer), 2668–2649 BCE • King of Egypt during Dynasty 3; ordered the Step Pyramid, the first true pyramid in Egypt, to be built by his architect Imhotep

Harkhuf (HAR-khoof), about 2278–2184 BCE • Egyptian explorer; lived during time of King Pepi II during Dynasty 6

Hatshepsut (hat-SHEP-soot), 1498–1483 BCE • Female king of Egypt; ruled in place of her stepson, Thutmose III, for nearly 20 years

Herodotus (huh-RAH-duh-tus), about 485–425 BCE • Greek historian; known as the "Father of History"

Homer, about 750 BCE • Greek poet; author of the *Iliad* and the *Odyssey*

Imhotep (im-HOE-tep), about 2668–2649 BCE • Egyptian architect and physician; designed and built the Step Pyramid for Pharaoh Djoser during Dynasty 3; worshipped as a god of healing by later Egyptians

Josephus (jo-SEE-fus), about 37–100 CE • Jewish general turned historian; wrote *Antiquities of the Jews*, *The Jewish Wars*, and *Against Apion*

Khufu (COO-foo), 2589–2566 BCE • King of Egypt during Dynasty 4; known to the Greeks as Cheops (KEY-ops); built the first of the three large pyramids (Great Pyramid) at Giza outside of modern-day Cairo

Manetho (MAN-eh-tho), 3rd century BCE • Egyptian priest and historian; first divided Egypt's pharaohs into dynasties

Menes (MEN-ease), about 3150–3050 BCE • Probably the same person as Narmer, king of Egypt during Dynasty "0," but possibly a legendary figure

Menkaure (MEN-ka-ray), 2532–2504 BCE • King of Egypt during Dynasty 4; built the third (and smallest) of the three large pyramids at Giza outside of modern-day Cairo; known to the Greeks as Mycerinus (my-sir-EE-nus)

Narmer, about 3150–3050 BCE • King of Egypt during Dynasty "0;" unified the two halves of the country (Upper Egypt and Lower Egypt)

Neferhotep (nef-er-HOE-tep) **I**, 1741–1730 BCE • King of Egypt during Dynasty 13, in the time of the Second Intermediate Period

Nefertiti (nef-er-TEE-tee), about 1350–1334 BCE • Queen of Egypt; wife of King Amenhotep IV/Akhenaten; known for her beauty; perhaps the power behind the throne

Pepi (PEH-pee) **II**, 2278–2184 BCE • King of Egypt during Dynasty 6; ruled for about 90 years

Piye (PEE-yee), 747–716 BCE • King of Kush and then of Egypt; thought to be the first king of Dynasty 25; also known as Piankhi (pee-AHNK-ee)

Plutarch (PLOO-tark), 46–120 CE • Greek philosopher and biographer; wrote *Lives of the Noble Greeks and Romans*, containing biographies of famous men

Ptolemy (TALL-uh-mee) **II**, ruled 285–246 BCE • Greek king of Egypt; second ruler during the Macedonian dynasty; best known for establishing the great Library at Alexandria and building the Lighthouse (Pharos) at Alexandria, one of the Seven Wonders of the Ancient World

Ptolemy (TALL-uh-mee) **III**, ruled 246–222 BCE • Greek king of Egypt; third ruler during the Macedonian dynasty

Ptolemy (TALL-uh-mee) **V**, ruled 205–180 BCE • Greek king of Egypt; fifth ruler during the Macedonian dynasty

Ramesses (RAM-ah-seas) **II** or **Ramesses the Great**, 1279–1212 BCE • King of Egypt; fought against the Hittites; possibly king during the Israelite Exodus; ruled for nearly 70 years and had many wives, concubines, and children

Ramesses (RAM-ah-seas) **III**, 1182–1151 BCE • King of Egypt; successfully defended the country against the invading Sea Peoples, among whom were the Philistines

Scorpion, about 3150 BCE • King of Egypt during Dynasty "0," before Narmer unified the two halves of the country

Senwosert (SEN-whe-sert) **I**, 1971–1926 BCE • King of Egypt; second ruler during Dynasty 12; also known as Senusret (SEN-use-ret) I

Seqenenre (seck-EN-en-re), about 1663–1570 BCE • King of Egypt during Dynasty 17; fought against the foreign Hyksos; killed in battle

Sinuhe (SIN-oo-way), about 1991–1926 BCE • Egyptian character, possibly fictional; story of his wanderings and life takes place during the reigns of Kings Amenemhet and Senwosert

Sostrates (SAUCE-trah-tees), 3rd century BCE • Greek architect; best known for designing and building the great Lighthouse (Pharos) at Alexandria, one of the Seven Wonders of the Ancient World, for King Ptolemy II

Strabo (STRAY-bow), about 63 BCE–21 CE • Greek geographer; wrote *Geographia*, a description of the world as known during his time

Thutmose (TUT-moze) **II**, 1518–1504 BCE • King of Egypt during Dynasty 18; best known as the husband of Hatshepsut and father of Thutmose III

Thutmose (TUT-moze) **III**, 1504–1450 BCE • King of Egypt during Dynasty 18; stepson of Queen Hatshepsut, who ruled in his place for nearly 20 years; fought against the Canaanites at the Battle of Megiddo, the first recorded battle in history

Thutmose (TUT-moze) **IV**, 1419–1386 BCE • King of Egypt during Dynasty 18; ordered the Dream Stela inscribed, to record a dream he had while sleeping between the paws of the Great Sphinx at Giza outside of modern-day Cairo

Tiy (tee), about 1386–1349 BCE • Egyptian queen; married to Amenhotep III of Dynasty 18; daughter of a nobleman named Yuya and his wife Tuya; had at least six children, including the future Amenhotep IV/Akhenaten

Tutankhamen (toot-an-KAH-mun), 1334–1325 BCE • King of Egypt during Dynasty 18; best known as the "boy king"; his tomb, filled with fabulous treasures, was discovered by British archaeologist Howard Carter in 1922

Wenamun (WEN-ah-mun), about 1098–1070 BCE • Egyptian character, possibly fictional; story of his journey to the cities of Dor and Byblos, in what are now modern Israel and Lebanon, takes place at the end of the New Kingdom Period

SOME PRONUNCIATIONS

Abu Simbel (a-BOO SIM-ball)

Abydos (a-BEE-dos)

Avaris (a-VAR-is)

Babylon (BA-bi-lun)

Canaan (KAY-nun)

Cyprus (SIGH-prus)

Euphrates (yoo-FRAY-teez) River

Giza (GHEE-zah)

Hattusa (HAH-too-sa)

Hermopolis (her-MAH-po-lis)

Hieracleopolis (HERE-a-klee-AH-po-lis)

Hierakonpolis (HERE-a-kon-po-lis)

Knossos (KA-naw-sus)

Lachish (LAH-heesh)

Megiddo (meh-GHEE-dough)

Mycenae (my-SEE-nigh)

Nekhen (NEH-ken)

Nubia (NOO-bee-uh)

Qadesh (Ka-DESH)

Sinai (SIGH-nigh)

Thebes (THEE-bz)

Tigris (TIE-griss) River

Ugarit (OO-gar-it)

ITALY

•Rome

GREECE

Athens•

Mycenae •

Mediterranean Sea

AFRICA

0   400 mi

0   600 km

THE ANCIENT EGYPTIAN WORLD

Black Sea

ASIA

• Hattusa

• Troy

ANATOLIA

MESOPOTAMIA

• Ugarit

Tigris River

Euphrates River

CYPRUS

• Qadesh

• Babylon

ssos

CRETE

CANAAN

• Megiddo

• Dor

• Lachish

Alexandria •

Nile Delta

• Avaris

Lower Egypt

Giza •

Memphis •

Hieracleopolis •

Sinai

EGYPT

Hermopolis •

Upper Egypt

• Amarna

Nile River

• Badari

Abydos •

Red Sea

ARABIA

• Thebes

Nekhen
(Hierakonpolis) •

Abu Simbel •

NUBIA

KUSH

CHAPTER 1

YOU RULE
THE GEOGRAPHY OF EGYPT

PHARAOH WHO?

Today we call all Egyptian kings "pharaohs," but ancient Egyptians didn't use the term until the 20th dynasty, from 1185 to 1070 BCE. The name comes from the Egyptian *per-ao*, or "great house," and over time came to mean the one who lived in the great house—the king.

Imagine you are the king of Egypt. Strut about a bit, you can. After all, you're the supreme ruler—the Pharaoh, the Great One. You command armies. If you say fight, they fight to the death. You have thousands of servants—a few just to fan you with ostrich feathers when you're feeling a tad overheated. Your brothers and sisters, parents, teachers, and friends have to do what you order. YOU have inherited the right to make laws and dole out punishments. They had better behave. When you walk by, people fall to their knees and press their noses into the dirt. Some tremble when you pass—who knows what you might say to the gods the next time you speak to them? The crops grow because you say so. The Great River flows because you convince the gods it must. Now imagine wielding all that power when you are only six years old. That's how old you would be if you were the Pharaoh Pepi II in Egypt 4,000 years ago.

If you were Pepi II, your kingdom would have looked a lot like the barren, red landscape of Mars if it weren't for one thing— the Great River, a river we now call the Nile. Flowing north, the Nile cuts through the deshret, or the red land. Limestone cliffs rise above the river like castle walls. The ancient Egyptians said the gods put

In this statue, Pepi II sits regally, wearing the royal headdress. He is carved to look like a miniature adult, but even kings sit on their mothers' laps when they are young. Some scholars believe Pepi II ruled for 94 years—the longest reign in Egyptian history.

those cliffs there to protect them. In fact, your entire kingdom is surrounded by natural barriers that protect it. To the east and west, the desert keeps out invaders. To the north, before the Nile dumps into the sea, it branches out into a triangle of marshland we call the Delta (it would be hard for your enemies to march through a swamp). And to the south the Nile protects your kingdom again, this time with a series of rocky rapids called the Cataracts.

Without the Nile you wouldn't have much of a kingdom to rule. Strutting might seem a bit silly. Egypt would be home to nothing more than a few wandering bands of nomads passing through the red land, dusty and dragging from the relentless heat, in search of the rare oasis. The Nile, however, the glorious Nile, brought a narrow band of life to Egypt. It carried rich, black dirt and spread it over the floodplains, creating fields for the Egyptians to plant their seeds. The Egyptians called it khemet—the black land. The change from red land to black land was so abrupt you could straddle the border, standing with one foot in red earth and the other in black.

The ancient Egyptians knew that without the Great River they would have no villages, no fields of wheat, and no cattle. To them the water was sacred. They believed it flowed from paradise and could heal the sick. They wrote songs to the Nile—praising its life-giving force. *The Hymn to the Nile* began "Hail to thee O, Nile!" and praised the Great River for coming "to give life to Egypt." It may seem as if the ancients got carried away with their praise when they sang, "If you cease your toil and your work, then all that exists is in anguish." But if the Nile did "cease its toil," the people would starve. Maybe they weren't so carried away after all.

Life in Egypt revolved around the Great River. Our seasons come and go, marked by weather changes, but not so in Egypt, where the sun always shines. In Egypt the seasons were marked by changes in the Nile. The first of the three seasons began in July. Egyptians called it akhet. During akhet, heavy rain in Ethiopia poured down from the highlands, swelling streams that fed the Nile. The banks of the

THAT'S ONE GIANT LETTER!

The fourth letter of the Greek alphabet, delta, is shaped like a triangle. Early in the sixth or fifth centuries BCE, Greek geographers named the triangle of land in Egypt where the Nile fans out into several smaller rivers and then flows into the Mediterranean Sea after their own letter "delta" because of its similar shape. By 450 BCE, the Greek historian Herodotus writes about Egyptians living "in that region which is called the Delta."

The Hymn to the Nile, about 2100 BCE

The green of the Nile Valley contrasts dramatically with the sandy desert. After the summer's torrential rainfalls on the Ethiopian highlands, the swollen Nile sweeps into the Nile Valley, flooding it with fertile soil and water.

MEANWHILE IN ETHIOPIA...

Ancient Egyptians kept such good flood records that scientists today use their data to better understand rainfall patterns. Weather forecasters study a phenomenon called El Niño. El Niño is a disruption in ocean currents that affects rainfall. It happens to cause droughts in Ethiopia. Rainfall in Ethiopia determines the flood levels of the Nile.

Nile overflowed. Flooding may not sound like a good thing, but to the Egyptians it was a very good thing. Those floods left behind that black earth for planting. During the floods, farmlands were covered with water. Everyone uneasily watched the water rise. Would there be enough water? Would the Nile bring enough of that rich, black earth for farmers to plant their seeds? Or would there be too much water? Would whole villages be washed away? It was a delicate balance. If you were the supreme ruler, it would be your job to work it out with the gods so that things went well. You worked with Hapi, the god of the Great River, and more importantly, with the god in charge of the floods, the one with the ram's head—Khnemu. It was your job to be sure there was *ma'at*, or balance—not too much, not too little.

The Egyptians watched the flood levels obsessively. They measured the water and recorded it. They compared their measurements to the good years. They compared their measurements to the bad years. Everywhere you went, people would have had an opinion on this year's flood level. People talked in the market place. People talked along the roads, over dinner, while washing clothes at the riverbank. Would this be a good year? Would the granaries be full? Or would this be a bad year? Would they suffer the anguish they sang about in *The Hymn to the Nile*?

At first the Egyptians simply marked the riverbank to measure the height of the Nile. But it wasn't long before the Egyptians invented measuring devices. We call them nilometers. Some looked like a giant yardstick made from marble. Other nilometers were even more elaborate. Workers dug staircases into wells and erected engraved pillars marked to gauge how high the water rose.

After the flood months, when the water finally receded and left behind rich, black earth, farmers scattered their seeds, the first of several plantings. The second season—peret—had begun. Farmers lifted water from the steady flowing river with shadufs, devices that looked like catapults. With a bucket for dipping on one end of a pole, and a counterweight to make lifting easy on the other, the shadufs creaked and groaned while farmers raised and pivoted the buckets to fill channels that snaked through their gardens.

Farmers tended their fields with care into the third season—shemu. During shemu the level of the Nile dropped, and many side channels dried up. The land parched and the desert seemed to close in. The red sands inched toward the villages. Near the end of shemu, Egyptians began to fret and worry. Would the Nile ever rise again? Had the gods forgotten to release the waters? They sang, "they dread him who creates the heat," and they sacrificed birds and gazelles for the return of the Nile's floodwaters. And then the cycle repeated. "Hail to thee, O Nile! Who... comes to give life to Egypt!"

> *The Hymn to the Nile*, about 2100 BCE

The shaduf has a bucket hanging from one end and a weight on the other. The farmer lowers the bucket into the Nile, and when it's full, he lets go and the counterweight lifts the heavy bucketful of water. Farmers still use shadufs today.

CAMEL-NOT

Although we picture camel caravans plodding across the sand dunes of the Egyptian desert, Harkhuf and his fellow traders traveled with donkeys. Camels weren't used to carry goods and people until very late in the sixth century BCE, nearly 2,000 years after Harkhuf's time.

Most Egyptians centered their lives around the Nile, but a few explored the countries surrounding Egypt. When Pepi II was nearly nine years old, he wrote to a man who had started his career when he was a young boy just like Pepi II. The man's name was Harkhuf. Harkhuf came from a family of explorers and had traveled with his father before making journeys on his own. Harkhuf led donkey caravans south across the desert to explore inner Africa. The details of Harkhuf's journeys are engraved just to the right of the entrance to his tomb located near the First Cataract of

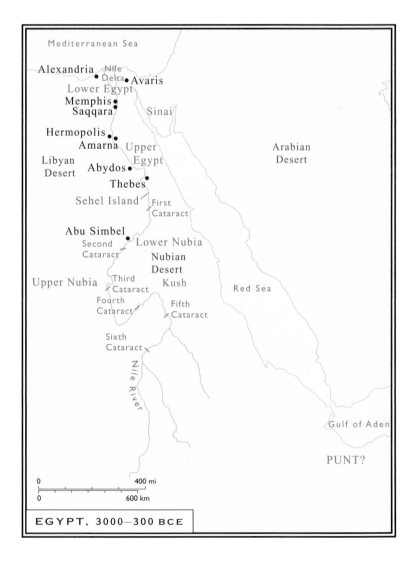

EGYPT, 3000—300 BCE

Priests anxiously watched the markings on nilometers such as this one to see how high the floodwaters would rise and compare that height with records of good years and bad. Later, tax rates were determined by the height of the yearly flood—then it was the tax collectors eagerly watching.

the Nile in Aswan. The long inscription begins high overhead on a chalkboard-sized area of the wall and continues down to waist level. Harkhuf begins his inscription with a little bragging about how he behaved in life. "I was excellent," he says, and goes on to tell of how his family loved and praised him. He writes about returning with 300 donkeys loaded with gifts for the Pharaoh. How would you like someone bringing you 300 donkeys loaded down with gifts, O Great One?

Clearly, Harkhuf is proud of a letter written to him by the boy-king Pepi II. The letter would have turned to dust long ago if Harkhuf hadn't been so honored by it that he carved it in stone. The letter from Pepi II is addressed to Harkhuf, calling him the chief of the desert rangers, the caravan conductor, and is dated: "Royal seal, year 2, third month of the first season, day 15." This shows us that Pepi II wrote to Harkhuf toward the end of the flood season in the second year of his reign, about 2276 BCE. The letter has tones of the royal-ness Pepi II must have been developing even at his young age, but it also shows that when you're only eight years old, it's hard to escape being a kid—even if you are a supreme ruler.

Pepi II wrote that he knew Harkhuf spent day and night with the caravan "doing that which thy lord desires, praises and commands." Not bad to have everyone running around trying to please you when you are barely nine. "Thy lord" has a nice ring to it, too.

❝ Harkhuf's tomb inscription, Aswan, about 2250 BCE

❝ Harkhuf's tomb inscription, Aswan, about 2250 BCE

❝ Harkhuf's tomb inscription, Aswan, about 2250 BCE

" Harkhuf's tomb inscription,
Aswan, about 2250 BCE

" Harkhuf's tomb inscription,
Aswan, about 2250 BCE

Despite all his power, Pepi II was still a young boy after all, and it was impossible for him to keep the excitement out of his letter. He had learned that Harkhuf was bringing home someone from the fabulous race of short people called pygmies. The talents of this particular dancing pygmy were so amazing that he was said to perform "the dance of the gods." Imagine waiting for someone *that* entertaining to arrive. Pepi II was having a little trouble waiting. "Come north to the Palace at once! Drop everything—hurry and bring that pygmy you have brought, alive, happy and well, for the divine dances, to gladden the heart, to delight the heart of the king who lives for ever!" (There's another kingly bonus—living forever.)

Pepi II wanted to be sure the dancing pygmy arrived unharmed. He ordered:

> get trusty men to stand around him on the gangplank—don't let him fall in the water! When he goes to bed at night, get trusty men to lie all round him in his hammock. Inspect him ten times a night! My majesty longs to see this pygmy more than all the treasure of Sinai and Punt!

Despite Harkhuf's major expeditions and all the riches he and other traders brought back to Egypt—from Nubia with all its gold, Sinai with all its turquoise, and Punt with all its incense—it was this dancing pygmy that captured the heart of Pepi II. And the letter written by the boy-king remained so important to Harkhuf that at the end of his days he chose to record it on his tomb. If you were the supreme ruler of Egypt 4,000 years ago, what kinds of letters would you write? What songs would you sing to the Nile? Think about it while your servants fan you with ostrich feathers. But you might want to be careful how you order your teachers around.

Harkhuf the explorer hikes with his walking stick on his tomb wall. When Harkhuf traveled, he preferred to use the safe desert routes. If his needs for food and water forced him to travel near the Nile, he hired soldiers to protect him from robbers.

CHAPTER 2

WRITTEN IN STONE
THE FIRST KING

I f you had an important story to tell, but most of your audience couldn't read, you might tell the story by drawing it in pictures. If you wanted the story to last a very long time, you might draw those pictures in stone. That's what an Egyptian storyteller did, and his work has lasted more than 5,000 years. It's the story of the first king of Egypt. And the stone is called the Palette of Narmer.

Long before the first king, before there were people of great power, before there were towns to lead, before there were villages with headsmen, the people of Egypt lived like all prehistoric peoples. They lived in small groups on the move. They followed the food.

Ten thousand years ago the area around the Nile hadn't dried up into desert yet. Rain fell more often and fields of grass grew. Elephants plodded about, flapping their ears in the heat. Giraffes nibbled on thorny trees. Vultures rode the warm air currents in search of something dead to eat. The people of Egypt hunted gazelle and dug root vegetables.

By 6,000 years ago, the people of Egypt had begun to herd cattle. When the Nile swelled and flowed over its banks, the people would follow their cattle away from the river. Extended families sometimes joined other groups while the cattle munched in the grasslands. By the end of summer, the heat and the lack of rain shriveled the grass, and the herders brought the cattle back to the edge of the floodplain—back to the Nile. They planted seeds and grew an early form of wheat called emmer. They grew peas, barley, and melons.

Small villages began to crop up along the Nile, just out of reach of the floodwaters. When the people argued, someone from the group would step in to solve the problem. Pretty soon they would look to that person to solve all of the problems. Power was born.

A farmer urges his animals to pull the plow while his wife follows, dropping seeds. Many early peoples believed the act of painting or carving was magical. Would drawing the trees loaded with fruit make the harvest bountiful?

Five thousand years ago some villages grew very large, and their headsmen grew very powerful. Two villages in particular had grown so large that we would call them towns: Nekhen in the south and Tjeni in the north. Location, location, location—it was all about location even then. Nekhen was the gateway to gold. This southernmost town of the Nile Valley was closest to the Nubian gold mines. Gold made Nekhen fat and prosperous.

Tjeni in the north was also a gateway. This town developed across the Nile from where the cliffs pinched the river into a narrow roadway. Tjeni controlled traffic on the Nile. And it was also here that tradesmen returning from the west entered Egypt. The goods they brought with them made Tjeni fat and prosperous. The wealth and power of Nekhen and Tjeni grew, and when it did, their leaders grew wealthy and powerful, too.

Nothing says wealthy like *things*. The rarer something is, the more exotic and the finer the quality, the louder it shouts about its owner, "Look at me, I'm rich and powerful,

I have all these fabulous things!" Artists no longer had to squeeze their craft making into what time they had left after tending their garden and milking their cows. People would gladly trade whatever the artist needed for the artist's talents. And now enough people lived in one spot to keep the artist busy all year.

For artists location meant something, too. One of the best locations for an artist in ancient Egypt was near a cemetery. The more power people had in life, the more fantastic their burial had to be. The dead were steady customers. Artists sculpted stone vases, molded clay figures, crafted gold jewelry, and carved stone palettes for the tombs of the rich and famous.

TOPSY-TURV

One ancient name for Egypt, "The Two Lands," comes from the fact that the country was once divided into two parts. Upper Egypt was "higher up" (in elevation) and Lower Egypt was closer to sea level. That can feel topsy-turvy to modern map readers who think of north as the upper part of the map and south as the lower part of the map. These differences in elevation cause the Nile to be one of the few north-south rivers to flow from the south to the north (from high ground to low ground).

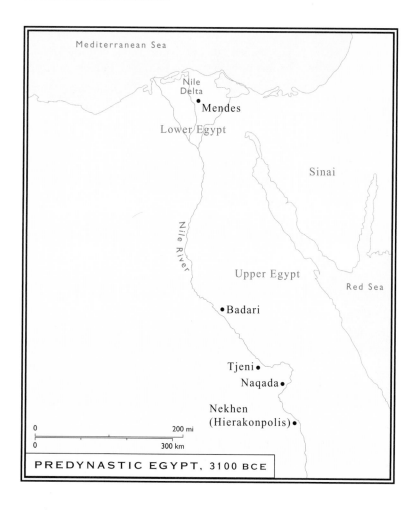

PREDYNASTIC EGYPT, 3100 BCE

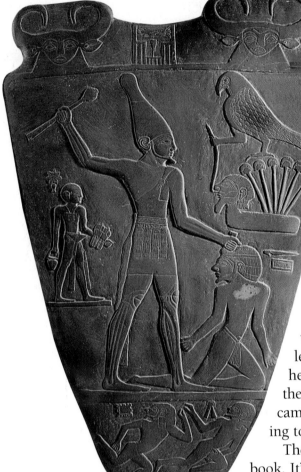

The chip-chip-chip of the stone carver would have been interrupted when the cattle herders returned with their herds at the end of summer. Eagerly, the carver would have inspected the green-gray siltstone the herders had collected in the Black Mountains and brought back with them. Ah, this stone would make a perfect turtle-shaped palette. This one definitely looks more like an antelope. The rounded one would be ideal for a hippo.

When the carver of the Narmer Palette saw that dark-green, nearly black, two-foot piece of stone, did he see a shield? Did he know in an instant that this particular fine-grained, flawless stone was fit for the first king? Did he dream about the story he would tell on the palette—the story of how the Two Lands came to be—the north and the south joining to become one?

The Narmer Palette is like a two-page comic book. It's in the shape of a shield and is carved on both sides. It tells the story of the unification of Egypt under one king—a king called Narmer. On one side of the palette, Narmer wears the White Crown of Upper Egypt, and on the other he wears the Red Crown of Lower Egypt. He's the first king to rule both.

On both sides of the palette, the very top has Narmer's name written inside a box called a serekh. Narmer means "angry catfish." King Angry Catfish has the head of a cow on either side of his name. Are these cow pictures meant to be the goddess Hathor? Many scholars think so. Ancient Egyptians thought the goddess Hathor was the king's mother and they usually drew her with her horns curled inward. Did this belief go all the way back to the very first king?

66 Narmer Palette, Hierakonpolis, about 3100 BCE

The legend of how a divided Egypt became one country is carved on the Palette of Narmer in the typical Egyptian style: Narmer's head, lower body, and legs are shown from the side, and the trunk of his body is shown from the front.

On the first page of our ancient comic book there are two scenes. The larger shows King Angry Catfish, or Narmer, about to smash the head of a man kneeling in front of him. The victim's name (or is it the name of a group of people?) is Wash and is written above his head. Could Wash be a leader that Narmer has conquered? Or is it symbolic of a whole tribe of people Narmer has beaten in battle?

More clues come from what is right in front of Narmer's face. The falcon perched on the reeds is no ordinary bird. He is Horus of Nekhen, the symbol of Egyptian royalty and protector of the king. Horus of Nekhen perches on reeds called papyrus. Each papyrus blossom is the Egyptian symbol for 1,000. The papyrus marsh with its 6,000 people is meant to be Lower Egypt. The meaning is clear. King Narmer—the king of Upper Egypt—has conquered and captured Lower Egypt.

That bowling-pin-shaped hat that King Catfish is wearing is the White Crown of Upper Egypt. The king is also wearing a bull's tail, which shows he is as strong as a bull. Behind Narmer there is a person carrying the king's sandals. He is much smaller in order to show that he isn't as powerful as Narmer. In the second scene those two men who look as though they are swimming are actually Narmer's fallen enemies sprawled helplessly inside their walled town. Narmer has won.

Page two of our comic book (otherwise known as "the back") is divided into three scenes. In the top scene Narmer is wearing the Red Crown of Lower Egypt. The Sandal Bearer is still following Narmer carrying his sandals, and Narmer is still holding his head-bashing mace, but instead of the hair of his enemy he holds a staff in his other hand. The staff is a symbol of royalty. He is parading with smaller,

These carved flat stones are called palettes because they were used to mix eye paint. Pigments were ground into dust on the stone and mixed with water in a round indentation, just as artists today would use palettes to mix their paints.

KING-FUSION

An ancient Egyptian legend claims that it was actually a king of Upper Egypt named Menes who united the Two Lands and was the first king of a unified Egypt. Some scholars say Menes was Narmer, others say Menes was Narmer's son, and still others think Menes is merely a legend.

less important people (everyone is less important than Narmer now) toward ten bodies with their heads cut off and placed between their legs. Like dogs with their tails tucked between their legs, these are the cowering, conquered enemies.

In the middle scene the elongated, entwined necks may look like two dinosaurs that got tangled, but they are supposed to be panthers and could symbolize the two parts of Egypt now joined together. If you draw a line through the middle, you can see that the two sides are mirror images. They balance. Narmer has brought harmony to Egypt.

The bottom scene on the palette shows a bull trampling a frightened foe. The bull is power. Narmer is powerful. He has conquered his enemies. They lie naked and helpless under his feet.

The palette shows Narmer victorious over the forces of evil. He has conquered chaos. He has given the Two Lands unity. The artist who carved the Palette of Narmer has told a dramatic story. Some say the Palette of Narmer is merely a legend. They say it wasn't the work of one king as powerful as a bull unifying Egypt, but that the Two Lands came together gradually over generations. Others say that Narmer was not the first king's real name. But one thing is certain—the story has survived for 5,000 years. It lives on the Palette of Narmer. It is written in stone.

This king wears the Red Crown of Lower (northern) Egypt. Most things in Egypt have gods associated with them, and crowns are no exception. The goddess of the Red Crown of Lower Egypt is Uto. On some crowns and headdresses, Uto takes the form of a cobra to spit venom at the king's enemies.

CHAPTER 3

STAIRWAY TO HEAVEN
THE OLD KINGDOM

❝ INSCRIPTIONS AT SEHEL AND EDWIN SMITH PAPYRUS

The king who followed Narmer was named Aha. Aha means "the fighter." That should give you a clue as to what life was like in Egypt after the "unification." Either no one had bothered to get the word out to the Egyptians that they were now unified, or not everyone bought into the deal, because for the next several hundred years, from about 3100 to 2670 BCE, the kings of Egypt spent most of their time squelching turf wars that flared up like forest fires. Every town with muscle and a headsman with attitude challenged the king. Each province struggled to hang on to its power. It took several hundred years and a king with a name that meant "divine body" to truly unify Egypt. A king named Djoser.

Egypt's list of kings is a long one. What makes the list run even longer is that most of the kings had several names. Take this one king, for example:

> Hor Ka-nakht tut-mesut, Nebti Nefer-hepu Segereh-tawy, Sehetep-netjeru Nebu, Hor Neb Wetjes-khau Sehetep-netjeru, Nesut Bit Nebkheperure, Sa re Tutankhamun Heqaiunushema.

In English, this name means:

> The Horus Strong Bull, Fitting from Created Forms, He of the Two Ladies, Dynamic of Laws, Who Calms the Two Lands, Who Propitiates all the Gods, the Golden Horus Who Displays the Regalia, Who Propitiates the Gods, King of Upper and Lower Egypt, Lord of Manifestations is Re, Son of Re, Living Image of Amun, Ruler of Upper Egyptian Iunu.

Fortunately for us, we know him as King Tut.

You can imagine how unwieldy the list became with more than 170 kings. Most of their names would have been lost if it weren't for an Egyptian priest and historian named Manetho, who lived in the third century BCE. He sorted out the entire disaster by collecting the records from various temples and putting them in order. To organize the list into something manageable, Manetho grouped the kings into thirty ruling families that we call dynasties.

Of course, once scholars start organizing there is no stopping them. In the 19th century, a German scholar decided to group the dynasties. Ordinarily this is where things fall apart. "Order" becomes so confusing you need to form a Ministry of Explanations for Scholarly Simplifications, or MESS, just to make sense of things. Mysteriously, something went terribly wrong and this time scholarly attempts to organize really did simplify things. The grouping of the dynasties goes something like this:

If Egypt was in a period of political stability with one king following the next fairly smoothly, the times were called "kingdoms." During these long stretches, Egypt enjoyed *ma'at*—the harmony of peace and prosperity that came from a strong central government. There are three such time periods, or "kingdoms"—the Old Kingdom, the Middle Kingdom, and the New Kingdom.

But, humans being human, sustaining peace forever (to date, at least) is impossible. So for those times in between when Egypt plunged into chaos—when the king's authority was challenged from outside Egypt and within—the groups of dynasties are called "intermediate periods." Although the dates of each kingship are not always clear or logical, and scholars argue over the specifics, the general design established by Manetho is still followed by historians today.

There are challenges to living in a country that is mostly desert. By the time the Old Kingdom rolled around, about 2700 BCE, Egyptians were up to meeting those challenges—the most obvious would concern water. Although the desert continually tried to push in on the farmland along the edge of the Nile, the Egyptians had learned how to push back. They coaxed the waters of the Nile inland, filling the buckets of their shadufs and emptying them into channels they had dug through their gardens. Not only were they irrigat-

While the boat owner sits in the back wrapped in his cloak, servants paddle the rivers of the Underworld. Wooden model boats like this one were often placed in Middle Kingdom tombs to provide the dead person with water transport in the afterlife.

ing their farmlands, they were expanding them. Farmers grew more food than the people could possibly eat. The king's granaries filled. The government organized and financed massive irrigation projects. When you grow more food than you can possibly eat you are left with something to trade with other nations—grain. What Egyptians didn't have they could now get through trade.

A challenge less obvious to those not used to surviving in a desert environment is the lack of wood. There are no tall trees in a desert. Actually, there are no trees at all, with the exception of what grew right along the edge of the Nile and in the occasional oasis. Egyptians needed wood—a lot of wood—especially for boats and coffins. They had their eye on the cedar that grew to the northeast, in the land that we now call Lebanon. It was ideal for both boats and coffins because cedar resists rot, and a rotting boat or a rotting coffin can be a problem. And so it began—we've got grain, we need wood, you've got wood, you need grain, let's trade. It was not much different, in principle, from trading baseball cards.

The richer the country, the more powerful its leader— and Egypt was becoming very rich indeed. The king became as distant and as "imperishable" as the stars—a god-king on earth, and in death truly divine. He was responsible for the stability, the order, the balance—*ma'at*. The simple tombs

STAR STRUCK

Inscriptions on the walls of Old Kingdom tombs compare kings to the "imperishable stars" over and over again. In one spell from the Pyramid Texts, the king asks for a ferry boat. "I will cross to that side on which are the Imperishable Stars, that I may be among them."

lined with brick and topped with a flat rectangular stone that had buried royalty in the past were no longer grand enough. What would the people think?

King Djoser wanted something that showed Egypt and the world just how powerful he was—showed this world and the next. He was fortunate enough to have a true genius for an architect—an architect capable of envisioning (and building) a tomb worthy of a god-king's passageway to the afterlife: a stairway to heaven. The architect's name was Imhotep and he built the first pyramid.

King Djoser must have traveled from the capital city of Memphis to the burial grounds at Saqqara now and again to inspect Imhotep's progress. King Djoser and Imhotep would have entered through a narrow passage positioned to capture the sun's first rays at daybreak. There were many false entrances along the nearly 20-foot-high wall surrounding the burial grounds, but only one way inside. They would have passed under the stone roof at the entrance carved to look like split logs and then through two giant doors permanently flung open. What did King Djoser think the first time he inspected the work site? How did he feel when he walked between the two parallel lines of stone columns carved to look like reeds bound in bunches? At the far end, the columns were placed closer and closer together to give the illusion of an even longer passageway. It must have seemed to him to stretch forever. This was no brick-lined hole in the ground. The burial complex was as big as 24 soccer fields.

King Djoser's Step Pyramid is the earliest known tomb made entirely out of stone. This was such an impressive feat that Djoser's architect Imhotep was granted "god" status after his death.

When King Djoser and Imhotep walked through the complex, winding their way through the columns carved with spitting cobras poised to protect the king, the clang of copper chisels would have made conversation difficult. Thousands of masons and sculptors worked the stone. It was the time of the inundation—the flooding of the Nile—and the farmers who were waiting for the waters to recede came to Saqqara to work for their king.

Imhotep would have carried drawings of his grand vision rolled in a papyrus scroll tucked under his arm. When the two walked through the complex they would have stopped here and there to watch an artisan at work. Surely, King Djoser would have felt the swell of pride

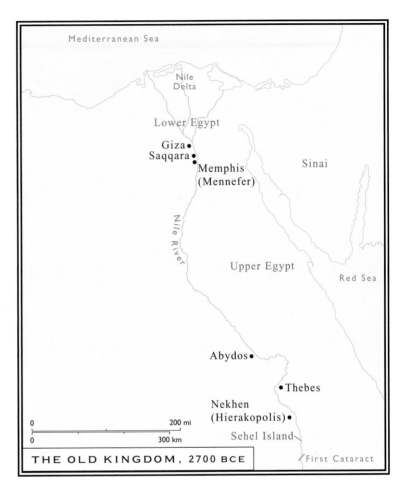

THE OLD KINGDOM, 2700 BCE

when he looked out over the sheer magnitude of the project. Only a great king could command such an endeavor—with so many meret—Egyptian peasants—working hard for the glory of their king.

The daily nilometer report would have filtered through the construction site, spreading from worker to worker, passed along with bread and beer. Were the waters as high as this time last year? Would there be enough? Too much?

Centuries later, a long inscription was carved into a granite stone on an island near the First Cataract. It claimed to record what King Djoser said after years of low floods, "I am distressed as I sit on the Great Throne...because the waters of the Nile have not risen to their proper height

Inscription, Sehel Island, near Aswan, about 2000 BCE

The story of the seven-year drought during King Djoser's reign is carved into a nine-foot-tall stone. "I was in mourning on my throne. . . . Those of the palace were in grief. . . . Temples were shut, Shrines covered with dust, Everyone was in distress. . . ."

for seven years. Grain is scarce, there are no garden vegetables at all. . . . The children are wailing."

But reports coming in on nilometer readings the years that King Djoser and Imhotep worked together on the burial complex indicated that the growing conditions would be good. The workers must have bustled about the burial complex with the energy that comes from high spirits.

Would Imhotep have saved the best for last? Would it have been at the end of the tour when he led King Djoser across the courtyard to the tomb? Finally they would have reached the base of the world's first pyramid and the world's first building constructed out of stone. Did Imhotep unroll a papyrus scroll and point to where he had planned the stacking of solid rectangles, each just a bit smaller than the one under it until a staircase rose 200 feet toward the sky? Would the construction noise have faded for King Djoser as he stood at the base of his eternal home? Even a god-king must feel awe at the sight of a structure larger than anything

The Edwin Smith Papyrus is a collection of 48 medical cases, each with a description of the injury, directions on how to examine the patient, a diagnosis, and a treatment. There were three possible diagnoses: for simple problems, "an ailment which I will treat," for trickier cases, "an ailment with which I will contend," and for incurables, "an ailment not to be treated."

built before it—a structure built not from mud brick that crumbles and decays with time, but built from stone, a monument built to be everlasting.

The laborers ten stories above King Djoser and Imhotep would have looked like ants pushing stones and fitting them into that highest step. Perhaps it didn't happen on a day that King Djoser was there, but it did happen all too often—a loose stone would fall. Dropping from that height even a pebble could be deadly. Scuffed loose, it would seriously wound someone below if it struck him. Imhotep had set up a small hospital for his workers. Anyone injured on the job would be cared for. Imhotep was not only an architect; he was a doctor as well. He wrote detailed directions on how to recognize an injury and how to treat it. The oldest known medical document is believed by some to have been written about 3000 BCE by Imhotep. It is called the Edwin Smith Papyrus, named after the Egyptologist Edwin Smith who bought the papyrus in 1862. One of the many instructions in the papyrus is what to do if a stone falls on a worker's head:

> Title: Instructions concerning a wound in his head penetrating to the bone of his skull.

> Treatment: . . . bind it with fresh meat the first day and treat afterward with grease, honey and lint every day until he recovers.

Today when archaeologists dig up the bodies of pyramid builders it is clear that many survived serious injuries thanks to Imhotep and his long list of cures. But many did not. And, during the Old Kingdom, life everlasting was not for the common man. He could only hope to play his part in the cycle of life and death by building a tribute to his king and in doing so add to the grandeur of Egypt.

" Edwin Smith Papyrus, 17th-century BCE copy of original estimated to have been written 30th century BCE

THANK *YOU,*
ROSETTA STONE
HIEROGLYPHS

" CLAY TABLETS
AND POTTERY FROM
ABYDOS, SATIRE
OF THE TRADES,
INSCRIPTION FROM
WADI HAMMAMAT,
AND THE ROSETTA
STONE

Humans are fascinated by firsts. Who was the first to step on the moon, the first to cross the sea—*the first to write?* Until recently, scientists thought the earliest writers were the Sumerians in Mesopotamia (which today is Iraq). But 300 pieces of pots no bigger than postage stamps are suggesting that writing began just as early in Egypt.

Scientists have been digging for decades in Abydos, an ancient royal cemetery west of the Nile, 300 miles south of Cairo. The ancient Egyptians buried their first kings in Abydos because they believed the mouth to the canyon there was the entrance to the next world. In a tomb that could be King Scorpion's, scientists are finding hundreds of pieces of pottery with some of the earliest writings in the world.

What words inspired some ancient Egyptian to invent writing? Were the words poetic? Were they wise? Did they reveal the true meaning of life? Did they point the way to the nearest watering hole? Nothing quite so meaningful—the inscriptions on the clay jars and vases are records of oil and linen deliveries. There was no money 5,300 years ago. Taxes were paid in goods. Sometimes they were paid with oil and linen. These very early written words were tax records. There is a saying that nothing in life is certain—except death and taxes. Maybe it's fitting that some of the earliest writings are tax records found in a cemetery.

We take writing for granted. In those first school years we carefully learn to draw the letters. We recite the sound each letter makes. But suppose no one had written before us, no teacher to show us what a letter looks like, no sound to go with it. How would you begin to write? The Egyptians began with pictures.

" Clay tablets from Abydos, about 3100 BCE

" Pottery from King Scorpion's possible tomb, Abydos, about 3100 BCE

At first the pictures stood for the real thing. A picture of the sun meant "the sun." As you can imagine, being able to write about only objects is limiting. How would you write the word "hot"? There is no object named "hot." So the pictures began to stand for ideas related to the object. A picture of the sun might mean light, or day, or—hot. It wasn't long before this was limiting, too. How would you write the word "belief"? What object could you draw that is related to the word belief? But if the objects could also represent a *sound*, then you could write "belief" as a picture of a bee followed by the picture of a leaf and the reader would be able to figure it out. (This example is an English word. The word for belief in Egyptian would be different, of course.)

It wasn't long before there were hundreds of symbols. Reading them was as complicated as writing them because Egyptian writers, called scribes, sometimes wrote right to left, sometimes left to right, and sometimes top to bottom (but never bottom to top). The only clue to which direction

MEANWHILE IN PAKISTAN...

In 1999, archaeologists on a dig in Harappa, Pakistan, found markings on pottery from 5,000 years ago. These plant-shaped symbols may be as old as the earliest examples of writing found in Egypt and Mesopotamia.

Some hieroglyphs stand for names, such as the name of Senwosret I repeated inside the ovals in this inscription. His name means "the Ka of Re comes into being." Other hieroglyphs stand for sounds. The squiggly line is a picture of rippling water and stands for the sound of the letter n.

hieros + *glyphe* = "sacred" + "carving" The Greeks called the Egyptian writing symbols hieroglyphs because they saw them carved into the walls of temples and other sacred places. }

you should be reading the inscription was the way the animals and people faced. You read toward the faces.

There was no punctuation. There were no periods or question marks so that the reader would know where one sentence ended and the next began. Not even a space between words helped to make the meaning clear. And if that doesn't complicate things enough, the fact that vowels were not used does. Imagine not being able to write a vowel, or should we write mgnntbngllwdtwrtvwl, or worse yet, lwvtrwtdwllgnbtnngm?

To the ancient Egyptians the written word was more than just a few scratches in clay. To them, once written, words had an eternal life—a voice. They could even be dangerous. For protection the picture of a crocodile was often drawn with a spear through it, or the snake drawn with its head chopped off. Imagine being afraid to write the word "beast" because you believed it could come to life and get you—talk about nightmares!

Egyptians called their writing *medu neter*, which means "words of god." Thousands of years later the Greeks named these writings **hieroglyphs**, which means "sacred carvings," because they found them covering temples and tombs.

Very few people in ancient Egypt could read and write, perhaps only 1 percent of the population. Imagine being one of the few who possessed the power to give a word life. Imagine being the keeper of the "words of god." The scribes shared this mysterious skill with rulers and gods.

Learning hieroglyphs wasn't easy. There were more than 700 signs to memorize. It took students years to master them. While other children were outside playing, the stu-

Scribes prepared their paints and then poured them into the inkwells on these palettes, dipping reed pens into the watery mix. The palettes were portable for business travel.

dents studying to be scribes spent their days bent over pieces of pottery, drawing and re-drawing the hieroglyphs. Students erased their work with a wet rag and started again until they had pleased their teachers.

If the students' minds began to wander, the teacher would remind them with words like these in the *Satire of the Trades*, "I would have you love writing more than your mother and have you recognize its beauty." If the students continued to misbehave, the teacher might warn them about other professions like the "coppersmith at his toil at the mouth of his furnace his fingers like crocodile skin his stench worse than fish eggs." Or the gardener who carried a pole across his shoulders "and there is a great blister on his neck, oozing puss." Maybe then, practicing hieroglyphs wouldn't seem so bad. The students might even agree with the teacher that "it is greater than any profession, there is none like it on earth."

Once the scribes' schooling was done it was time to become an apprentice and to learn even more about the craft by serving a working scribe. We know from an inscription on a statue that a scribe named Bekenkhons spent 11 years as an apprentice in the royal stables after going to school for 4 years at the temple of Mut at Karnak. There were plenty of job opportunities for scribes. Everything from personal letters to military secrets to magic spells was written by the scribes. Scribes calculated how many bricks it would take to build a wall, and how many loaves of bread it would take to feed the bricklayers. Scribes wrote out healing directions for doctors. They recorded births and deaths. Anything anyone wanted or needed written down required a scribe.

❝ *Satire of the Trades* or *Instruction*, about 1991–1782 BCE

Scribes record the year's harvest with their reed pens. Ancient Egyptians were careful record keepers, but in triplicate?

Over time, the slow-to-write hieroglyphs were replaced by an easier system of writing. Scribes still used the sacred way of writing on temples and tombs, but for everyday writing they used a shorthand they called *sesh*, which means "writing for documents." Later, the Greeks named this writing hieratic.

Documents were often written on paper made from the papyrus plant. Papyrus makers would peel the skin off the triangular stem of the papyrus reed, then slice the stem into thin strips. They laid the strips next to each other overlapping slightly, then arranged another layer on top going in the opposite direction. After covering the reed strips with linen, they pounded the sheet with a mallet. The crushed reeds oozed sticky papyrus sap. When dry, the sap glued the strips together. The sheets were most often used like the pages of a book, but if the scribes wanted long rolls, they glued the ends of the sheets of paper together with flour and water paste. Scribes wrote on the papyrus sheets with pens that looked like paintbrushes. They dipped their brushes in water, then rubbed the brush on a cake just as you mix watercolors. Black cakes were charcoal often made from the soot on cooking pots. Red cakes came from the red earth of the desert.

Hieroglyphs are everywhere in Egypt. There are even markings like ancient graffiti on the stones along travel routes. Some are very old like this inscription written nearly 4,000 years ago at a quarry in the mountainous desert: "I was commander of the troops... in this highland, equipped with water skins, baskets,...and every fresh vegetable of the South. I made its valleys green, and its heights pools of water; settled with children throughout...." And some are more recent, like the "thank-you note" that a group of priests wrote in 196 BCE to their 13-year-old Pharaoh Ptolemy V for making it a law that their temple receive money. They carved the law and their appreciation on polished black stone. They wrote the thank you note three ways—in hieroglyphs, demotic, and Greek.

For more than 3,000 years, the sons and the occasional daughter of the rich and the royal studied to become

" Inscription, Wadi Hammamat, about 1930 BCE

scribes. It was a profession for the privileged. But over time, fewer and fewer scribes learned the ancient sacred symbols. The Greek alphabet found its way into Egyptian writing and even vowels became visible. Eventually, there was no one left who knew how to read those first words drawn in pictures.

In modern times, the curious drawings taunted scholars. The mysterious history of ancient Egypt was right there in front of them. If only someone could read it. The carvings circling temple columns, the paintings coloring coffins, the words written on tomb walls waited in silence for someone to crack the code. Who would be first to figure out what the ancients had written?

In 1799 the French army was in Egypt as part of Napoleon's grand plan to conquer the world. His engineers were rebuilding an old fort along the branch of the Nile called the Rosetta. The men had torn away one wall and were clearing the rubble when they found a gleaming black stone carved in three different scripts. Even though the engineers could not read the words, they knew the stone must be important. Napoleon sent artists to make copies of the text carved in the stone and the copies were sent to scholars all over Europe.

The slab of black stone that the priests had carved the thank-you note into 2,000 years before became known as the Rosetta Stone. Scholars translated the Greek right away, but no one could read demotic or hieroglyphs. How did those curious carvings work?

The first real breakthrough came from an Englishman named Thomas Young. By the time Young was 2, he was reading. By the time he was 7, he was fluent in 3 languages. By the time he was 14, he was fluent in 12 languages. Young was sure he would be the first to crack the code. He discovered

The Rosetta Stone, about 196 BCE

The Rosetta Stone contains one of the first "presidential" pardons. Part of the text says, "those who were in prison and those who were under accusation for a long time, [King Ptolemy] has freed of the charges against them."

Ancient Egyptians drew an oval called a cartouche *around the names of kings, queens, and high-ranking officials. The cartouche magically protected the name on monuments.*

that the hieroglyphs for the 13-year-old Pharaoh Ptolemy's name were repeated six times inside little ovals that the French called *cartouches*, because they looked like the paper rolls, or cartouches, that the French stored their gunpowder in for their muskets. Young worked on the demotic lines and was able to figure out many words, but the hieroglyphs stumped him. It took another young genius, building on Young's work—a man named Jean François Champollion—to finally translate the entire Rosetta Stone.

A simple thank-you note written by grateful priests turned out to be the key that opened the Egyptian past for modern scholars. No longer would scholars have to settle for the Greek, Roman, or Hebrew version of Egypt's history. Egypt's own stories could now come to life. Maybe there is magic in the written word after all. To be on the safe side, let's *not* write the word for that hairy, scary thing that rhymes with "feast."

"*Happy is the heart of him who writes. . . . Be a scribe! Your body will be sleek, your hand will be soft. You will not be like a hired ox. You are one who sits grandly in your house: your servants answer speedily.*"

—Papyrus Lansing, a schoolbook by the royal scribe Nebmare-nakht, who lived between 1185 and 1070 BCE

CHAPTER 5

IT'S A GOD-EAT-GOD WORLD
EGYPTIAN RELIGION

❝ ANIMAL RE
AT SAQQARA, G
ABYDOS STELA,
PLUTARCH, AND
PYRAMID TEXTS

The ancient Egyptians had a god for everything. That palm tree set back from the Nile sprouting on the rise behind your cousin's house? It had a god. The make-up your father applied from his palette in the morning? It had a god, too. More than 2,000 names of gods have been found written in limestone, on papyrus, and scratched on mud-brick walls. Some gods were powerful and worshipped by many, and some were wispy spirits known to just a few. There were gods whose spirits lived inside real things, such as the Nile, the sun, the sky, and the earth. And there were gods for protection against dangers, such as the bites of crocodiles, scorpions, and snakes. There were gods who stood for learning—the art of music and medicine; and there were gods who stood for the learned—the scribes and the architects. You name it, the Egyptians had a god for it.

There were good gods and bad gods, and fierce gods to protect you from the bad gods. There were gods for the living and gods for the dead. Some gods were human, some were animal, and some were a little of both. The bulls of one breed were so sacred that they lived like kings, and when they died the Egyptians mummified them, just like they would a pharaoh. They covered the bulls in jewels and placed them in coffins carved out of solid blocks of granite each weighing 80 tons. These sacred bulls even had their own cemeteries. At a burial site at Saqqara archaeologists have found 24 bulls, each in an elaborately carved coffin.

The most important god in Egypt was the sun god. The Egyptians pictured the sun god pushing the sun across the sky just as the scarab beetles pushed tiny dirt balls across the ground. Every morning the Egyptians were grateful when the sun was born again like the tiny scarab eggs hatching in the dirt ball. And every evening when the sun

❝ Animal remains, Saqqara, about 612–30 BCE

In addition to bulls, the Egyptians also embalmed birds, such as this ibis.

Egyptians believed that the sky was an ocean of water. Stretched out in a push-up, Nut, the sky goddess, separates the watery sky from the earth.

set, they worried that an evil snake would swallow the sun as it passed through the Underworld.

Different towns in Egypt worshipped different gods. The leaders of the town would try to convince everyone that their god was the most powerful. If their god was powerful, it meant they were powerful, too. Before Upper and Lower Egypt were unified, each had its own capital with its own goddess. Upper Egypt's goddess looked like a vulture. Lower Egypt's goddess looked like a cobra. After Upper and Lower Egypt unified, the kings wore a crown with both a vulture and a cobra to symbolize the joining of the regions.

One of the pharaoh's most important jobs was to take care of the gods. If the gods were happy, the Egyptians figured they would be happy, too. The crops would grow, the Nile would flood to the right level, and Egypt would be at peace with its neighbors. Life would be in balance, or *ma'at*. The pharaohs built great temples to show respect to the gods. Inside each temple, in the innermost room, they placed a shrine. And inside the shrine, they kept a statue of the god for whom the temple had been built. Every day the priests served the statue as if it were alive.

One pharaoh, King Neferhotep (who ruled about 1741 to 1730 BCE), paid special attention to the temple at Abydos.

King Neferhotep wanted to be sure the priests were taking care of the statue exactly as they were supposed to take care of it. After all, those priests were the king's representatives. So if they displeased the gods, then the gods were displeased with the king as well. *Ma'at* would be thrown all out of whack.

On the road leading to Abydos, there was a stela, which is a slab of rock with inscriptions on it. The stela tells the story of King Neferhotep's concern over the spirit of the god Osiris, who lived in the statue, which lived in the shrine, which lived in the innermost room inside the temple at Abydos. According to the stela, King Neferhotep "desired to see the ancient writings." The ancient works were kept by the priests, "the real scribes of hieroglyphs, the masters of all secrets." King Neferhotep told the priests who watched over the ancient records that he planned a "great investigation" into the proper care of the statue of Osiris. The priests replied, "Let your majesty proceed to the house of writings and let your majesty see every hieroglyph."

King Neferhotep studied the ancient writings in the library. He learned how the gods were cared for from the beginning of time. He learned exactly what rituals pleased the gods. He decided that he should go to Abydos himself to explain to the priests what he had learned. King Neferhotep sent a messenger ahead telling the priests to bring the statue of Osiris to meet his royal barge on the Nile when he landed.

When King Neferhotep arrived near Abydos, the priests met him. The statue of Osiris had traveled with them in its shrine. The shrine had been placed in a cabin on a boat modeled after the boat that the Egyptians believed the gods

66 Great Abydos Stela, Abydos, about 1740 BCE

Scholars believe that the symbol called the ankh in the center of this stone slab is the origin of the much-later Christian cross. It also looks like a key—for ancient Egyptians, the key to eternal life.

used to navigate the stars. The boat rested across poles shouldered by a procession of priests.

On the seven-mile journey from the Nile to the temple, King Neferhotep was entertained by the priests, who acted out the Legend of Osiris. We know bits and pieces of the legend from inscriptions on the tomb walls and from songs such as the *Great Hymn to Osiris*. The most complete version of the legend, however, was written much later, probably in the first century CE, by the Greek historian Plutarch. The legend has been told in many ways. This is one version:

Osiris and Isis were two of the original nine gods. They were the children of the goddess of the sky and the god of the earth. Osiris became king of Egypt. He married the great love of his life, his sister Isis. His brother, Seth, was jealous. Seth wanted everything that Osiris had. He wanted to be king. He wanted his power. He wanted Isis. Seth pushed sibling rivalry into the evil zone. He plotted to destroy Osiris. Plutarch writes, "Seth secretly measured the body of Osiris and had made to the corresponding size a beautiful chest which was exquisitely decorated. He brought the chest to a banquet, and when the guests showed pleasure and admiration at the sight of it, Seth promised playfully that whoever would lie down in it and show that he fitted it, should have the chest as a gift." Then, in true Cinderella-and-the-glass-slipper fashion, everyone tried the coffinlike chest on for size. Some were so fat they couldn't squeeze

Plutarch, *Of Isis and Osiris*, about 45–125 CE

Say the right spell in the afterlife and this statue of Osiris would come to life. Osiris protects the spells inside the box on which he stands.

The falcon god Horus wears the crown of Lower Egypt. Egyptians believed gods ruled Earth before humans did. The first human kings were called "The Followers of Horus."

into the box. Others were so small they slid right out. But, finally, when Osiris tried the coffin, the fit was just right. Plutarch writes that Seth "ran and slammed the lid on, and after securing it with bolts from the outside and with molten lead poured on, they took it to the river and let it go to the sea..." Osiris drowned. Death came to Egypt for the first time.

" Plutarch, *Of Isis and Osiris,* about 45–125 CE

Seth enjoyed everything that once belonged to Osiris. But whereas Osiris was kind, Seth was cruel. There was no *ma'at* in Egypt with Seth in charge. There was war and hunger and lawlessness. Only Isis was unafraid of Seth. She found Osiris's body and turned herself into a bird and sang to him. In a fury, Seth cut Osiris into pieces and scattered him all over Egypt. Isis and her sister searched "in a papyrus boat, sailing through the marshes" for all his parts. They collected the pieces of Osiris, and with the help of Anubis, god of the dead, they sewed him back together.

" Plutarch, *Of Isis and Osiris,* about 45–125 CE

From a passage in the Pyramid Texts, we know that Isis and Osiris had a son who challenged Seth, "in the name of 'Horus the son who avenged his father.'" Each time Horus fought Seth to take back the throne, Isis protected him from injury with her power. In a final battle, Seth turned into a ferocious crocodile. But Horus managed to spear the crocodile, killing Seth. In the end, Horus restored *ma'at* to Egypt.

" Pyramid Texts, about 2375–2184 BCE

When the play was over, King Neferhotep and the procession had arrived at Abydos. Abydos was one of the most sacred places in ancient Egypt. One legend claims that Osiris himself is buried there. Another legend says the only part of Osiris buried at Abydos is his dismembered head.

Unlike today's religious buildings, in ancient Egypt temples were not open to the common people. Anyone entering

MULTI-PAPYRUS

Papyrus was not only used to make paper. Among other things boats, sandals, rope and mats were made from this versatile reed.

the temple had to be "pure" so as not to offend the god. To become pure, the priests bathed several times a day. Hair could carry dirt or worse, lice, so priests shaved their bodies every three days. They even pulled out their eyelashes. The common Egyptian could only catch a glimpse of the shrines as they were moved from place to place. When the priests

MAJOR GODS AND GODDESSES OF EGYPT

Amun	*Creator god, associated with fertility; sometimes pictured as a goose, but most often represented as a man*
Anubis	*Necropolis god, connected with mummification; usually has head of a dog or jackal*
Bastet	*War goddess; has head of a lioness or cat*
Hathor	*Goddess of women, also sky goddess, tree goddess, or necropolis goddess; has head of a cow or cow's horns, often with sun disk on head*
Horus	*Sky god; has head of a hawk, often with double crown*
Isis	*Wife of Osiris, guardian, and magician; often has hieroglyph of her name on her head*
Montu	*War god; often has head of a hawk, with sun disk and two plumes on top*
Neith	*Goddess of war and hunting; wears red crown or has two crossed arrows and shield on her head*
Osiris	*Ruler of the Underworld, god of dying vegetation, and husband of Isis; usually shown as a mummy and holding a scepter and wearing white crown with plumes and horns*
Ptah	*A creator god; the patron of all craftsmen, including architects, artists, and sculptors; frequently shown as a man dressed as a mummy, he built the boats for the souls of the dead to use in the afterlife*
Re	*Sun god; has head of a hawk, often with sun disk on head*
Seth	*God of disorder, deserts, storms, and war; usually has head of an unidentified animal*
Thoth	*God of writing and counting; has head of an ibis, often with moon crescent; sometimes depicted as a baboon*

brought the statue of Osiris to meet King Neferhotep, people would have lined the route, not only to see the priests sing, dance, and perform, but also to peek at the shrine.

The statues were kept inside the temples, in the innermost room. The priests didn't believe the statue actually *was* the god, but they did believe the god's spirit lived inside the statue. In the morning, the high priests would break the clay seal on the sanctuary door. They would chant and burn incense. A priest would gently wake the god by lighting a torch, symbolic of the sunrise. The priests bathed, dressed, and presented food to the statue. Then when the day's rituals were completed, the priests would back out of the room, smoothing away their footprints with a reed broom. The sanctuary doors were sealed so that the god could get a good night's sleep undisturbed.

Plucking out your eyebrows and eyelashes may sound painful, but being a priest had advantages. For one thing, you didn't have to pay taxes. All the priests except the highest order spent only three months of the year serving at the temples. The rest of the time they lived ordinary lives, working at their professions—scribes, artists, musicians. And even the highest priests had families outside the temples.

Abydos wasn't the only sacred site. There were many others throughout Egypt. Some temples were mortuary temples for dead kings, and others were built to honor a particular god. Some, like Abydos, were both. Abydos honored Osiris, and because Osiris was the King of the Dead, it also became an important burial ground.

For Egyptians, the stories about the gods were comforting and provided guidance in a world that was unpredictable and governed by forces they didn't understand. Horus watched over them in this life. Osiris watched over them in death. When their world was in turmoil, they believed it was Seth fighting with Horus that created the chaos. When all was well, they were sure that Horus had won the battle. They believed that one day Horus would defeat Seth in a smashing final combat. Then Osiris would be able to return to the world of the living and all sorrow would end. Until then, it was a god-eat-god world.

The Eyes of Horus are inscribed at the top of this stone slab. Horus, the god often shown as a hawk, has the eyes of a hawk—all seeing. The Eyes of Horus were often painted on the prows of ships to "see" the way.

ARCHAEOLOGIST AT WORK:
AN INTERVIEW WITH DAVID O'CONNOR

Professor David O'Connor's work is the stuff movies are made of—he digs in the city built to honor the King of the Dead. But Professor O'Connor's work isn't done on a movie set. The Egyptian desert poses challenges for even the hardiest adventurer. Since 1967 Professor O'Connor has met those challenges, excavating in Abydos, in Upper Egypt, so that we may have a better understanding of how the people in the Old Kingdom lived as far back as 5,000 years ago. David O'Connor is currently the Lila Acheson Wallace Professor of Ancient Egyptian Art at the Institute of Fine Arts, New York University. He was formerly Professor of Egyptology at the University of Pennsylvania.

When you were a kid did you know you would become an archaeologist?

Yes, quite early on I became very interested in archaeology and ancient civilizations. In fact, when I was a kid of about 9 or 10, living in Australia, I read about the ancient city of Babylon, which was in Mesopotamia. I built a large model of that city in a field next to our house. Then, because I had read that ancient cities were often attacked and burned by enemy soldiers, I burned the whole model down. Today, we call this experimental archaeology!

What drew you as a scholar to Egypt, more specifically Abydos?

What attracted me was the richness of its archaeology. If you are interested in the ancient Near East and ancient Africa as I was, among all those cultures, the archaeology of Egypt has survived much better than anywhere else in terms of monuments, art, and objects of daily life. And so Egypt is really the best place to try and reconstruct the ideas of very early people. Abydos attracted me as an archaeologist because it's a very important and mysterious site. That's what archaeologists like better than anything else. It's a mystery that needs to be solved. We knew Abydos was very important to the ancient Egyptians because some of their earliest kings were buried there. Later it became the center for the god Osiris, the king of the dead. That made Abydos very significant to all Egyptians. We knew these things from the work of earlier archaeologists at Abydos, but there were still many things about the site that were mysterious and unknown, and that's why we decided to go back there.

What time of year do you usually excavate?

In Egypt we prefer to excavate in the winter or the spring, because in the summer and the early autumn the weather is very, very hot. So it's difficult to work out of doors, which is what we do.

Is it ever dangerous or scary?

Working at Abydos. we do have to be careful to watch out for snakes, especially poisonous snakes and scorpions that can give you a very painful sting. Both of them live in or near the desert, and that's where our work is located. However, the good thing is we work there mostly in the winter and in the winter the snakes hibernate. They are not very active in the cooler weather. The same is true for scorpions.

The earliest excavators in Egypt took things without paying much attention to where they were found. When you excavate you take great care in mapping out where everything is found in relationship to everything else. Why is that important to do?

One of the first excavators of Abydos, William Petrie, set an example for the ones to follow. He is considered the founder of scientific archaeology in Egypt. We are careful about not just finding things, but where they were found. As at other archaeological sites in Egypt, we are very careful when we excavate buildings, or find objects, to record them in place. Just to give you an idea how seriously we take that, when we find a brick wall we actually draw in all the bricks, not just the wall. And the reason why we pay so much attention to where objects are found, or how they are located with regard to other objects or buildings, is because knowing this makes it much easier to understand how the objects were used and what the buildings were used for.

What is one of the most exciting discoveries you have made at Abydos?

Our most exciting discovery at Abydos was that of 14 full-size wooden boats, each one about 75 feet long and buried in the desert.

What were boats doing more than eight miles from the Nile?

The boats we found were far away from the Nile, buried in the desert, because they were intended not to be used on the river, but to be used in the afterlife, in the world of the dead. They had been buried at Abydos in order to be available for one of the early kings who had been buried there.

Why might a king bury boats with him?

Like a lot of things at Abydos, the use that might have been made of these boats by a dead king is mysterious. There are several possibilities. One is that the boats were imagined to deliver supplies to the dead king for all eternity. Another possibility, which we know from later ideas about the royal afterlife, is one in which the king himself sails in the boats through the world of the dead, just like the sun god was supposed to do.

These huge boats were made out of wood. Wood is scarce in the desert. Is there anything you can learn from finding out where the wood came from?

The kind of information we can get by identifying the wood or woods (there may be more than one) depends on the kind of wood the boats turn out to be made of. If it's a local wood, then it tells us about the Egyptians' own technology, but if it's an imported wood, like cedar from Lebanon, then we get important information about Egyptian early trading partners.

CHAPTER 6

IT'S A WRAP
MUMMIES AND THE AFTERLIFE

Mummies make terrific horror movie creatures, as the actor Boris Karloff did when he starred in the 1932 movie The Mummy. *What's spookier than a 3,000-year-old corpse suddenly coming to life?*

In monster movies the Mummy lurches forward, dragging his leg. Ancient Egyptians wouldn't have been scared by this stumbling bag of rags. In fact, they would probably have pointed and laughed, because every Egyptian knew mummies don't lurch. They don't drag their legs. They walk with the grace of an athlete, because in the Field of Reeds, which is where the dead lived, that limp would magically disappear. Deaf in one ear? No problem. Festering wound? No problem. Perfect health is yours in the Field of Reeds.

The Egyptians imagined that the Field of Reeds looked like home—only better. A gentle river meandered through fertile fields while munching cows looked on. The cows were fat and happy. They didn't even need to swish their tails, because there were no annoying flies in the Field of Reeds. The fields were always bursting with ripe foods ready to pick. No one was ever sick or hungry, and best of all, no one had to work.

The trick was getting in.

The Egyptians believed that everyone had three spirits—the Ba, the Ka, and the Akh. Each spirit played a different role when the body died. In its natural state, the Ba—the person's personality—looked like a bird with a miniature version of the dead person's head. After death the Ba lived in the tomb, but was free to come and go as it pleased. The Ba often went to the land of the living where it changed into anything it fancied.

The Ka, on the other hand, was stuck in the tomb. It had to stay with the body. In order to survive, the Ka needed to eat and drink. Friends and family of the dead person would bring offerings to the tomb for the Ka. They even brought clothing for it. The Ka needed the corpse, or the spirit would perish—and if it perished, good-bye Field of Reeds. In an emergency situation, the Ka could use a statue that looked like the deceased as a fallback body. Or it could even occupy a picture of the deceased on the tomb wall. Pharaohs paid artisans to recreate their images *everywhere*. A forgotten pharaoh was doomed. No sense taking chances.

The Akh was the spirit that represented immortality. It could shine with the stars at night and the sun in the day, or live forever in the Field of Reeds. The three spirits' main responsibility was to make sure that the dead person lived forever. Their job was to gain entrance to the Field of Reeds.

WORKING STIFF

No eternal bliss is complete without servants to attend to every whim. To do the work in the next world, stone or wooden figures were buried with the dead. These figures, called *shabti*, were statues of people performing chores such as farming and baking, each engraved with the spell that would make sure they did what they were supposed to do.

Step-by-step directions on how to make a mummy were painted on this stone coffin called a sarcophagus. In the top three panels, Anubis, the jackal-headed god, takes care of the deceased.

And here's where it got tricky, because entering the Field of Reeds was as challenging as any video game.

When a person died, his or her spirit took off toward the setting sun and entered the dangerous Underworld. After a long journey the spirits arrived at a labyrinth of gates and doors. The gatekeepers and the magical doors would quiz the spirits.

"I will not let you through me," says the jamb of the door, "unless you tell me my name."

"I will not open for you," says the bolt of the door, "unless you tell me my name."

There were many names to memorize in order to open the doors, names such as "She Who Licks Her Calves" and "He Who Cuts Up An Opponent" and "Toe of His Mother." Call one tormentor by the wrong name and you were condemned to haunt your own grave and wander the desert moaning through eternity.

With so much to lose, the Egyptians came up with a cheat sheet. During the Old Kingdom, only pharaohs could get into the Field of Reeds. Not wanting to risk forgetting a name or a spell, the kings had the answers to all the questions, along with all the magic spells, buried with them. We call the book of spells from the Old Kingdom the Pyramid Texts. During the Middle Kingdom, when the Field of Reeds was open to everyone, the spells were conveniently written on the sides of the coffins. We call those the Coffin Texts. In the New Kingdom the spells were written on scrolls and buried with the body. The words written during the New Kingdom are now known as the Book of the Dead. The Egyptians thought of every possible unpleasantness and wrote spells to protect against it. They even had a spell that prevented them from having to stand on their head and eat feces—or step in some. "What I detest is feces, and I will not eat it . . . and I will not touch it with my toes." Obviously the ancients weren't taking chances on anything less than a perfect afterlife.

The Pyramid Texts, the Coffin Texts, and the Book of the Dead all had the same purpose—turn the quiz into an open-book exam and guarantee that the spirits passed.

" Pyramid Texts, about 2375–2184 BCE

" Book of the Dead, about 1500–250 BCE

" Book of the Dead, about 1500–250 BCE

Once safely though the labyrinth of portals, the spirits entered the hall of judgment. Before 42 gods, the spirits declared their innocence to everything the Egyptians could think of. The cheat sheet helped them remember all the sins they didn't commit. The spirits addressed the gods one by one. Some of the gods had creepy names: Bone Breaker and Blood Eater, for example. Some gods had rather unusual names: Fiery Eyes, Hot Foot, and Pale One. Others had names that would make good video game demons: Demolisher, Lord of Truth, and the Accuser. Still others sounded a bit goofy, as if they were one of the Seven Dwarfs—Nosey, for example. The spirits had to remember which sin they denied to which god (with the help of their cheat sheet). Apparently being noisy was considered sinful. One of the denials was "O Water-smiter who came forth from the Abyss, I have not been loud voiced."

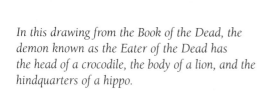 Book of the Dead, about 1500–250 BCE

If all went well in the hall of judgment, the spirits moved on to the final test—and this is where Anubis came in. Anubis had the body of a human and the head of a jackal. One of his official titles was "Lord of the Mummy Wrappings." It was Anubis who administered the final test. On one side of a balance scale, he would place the dead person's heart and, on the other, a feather that symbolized truth and justice. The god Thoth, who was the scribe of the gods, stood by with his pen ready to write down the test results. Would the heart weigh heavy with sin? Or would it balance with truthfulness and justice? If it balanced, the deceased was given a plot of land in the Field of Reeds. But if the balance tipped, the deceased met a very different fate. Near the scales a fierce monster called "The Eater of

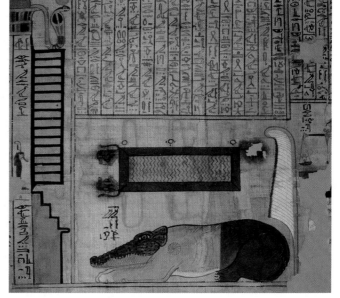

In this drawing from the Book of the Dead, the demon known as the Eater of the Dead has the head of a crocodile, the body of a lion, and the hindquarters of a hippo.

SACRED ANIMALS

For the Egyptians it was unthinkable that a sacred animal (or beloved pet) be left to rot. They mummified animals by the thousands—sometimes millions. At Tuna el-Gebel, the cemetery of Hermopolis, scientists have unearthed more than four million mummies of a storklike bird called an ibis.

the Dead" waited—and he was hungry. Anubis fed the Eater of the Dead the hearts of those who failed the final test. Without a heart, the dead person was doomed. Egyptians believed that the three spirits needed their *whole* body to live in the Field of Reeds. If they were missing any essential part, they would spend eternity as evil spirits haunting the living. Naturally, the living did everything they could to preserve the body.

In the beginning nature preserved the bodies. The Egyptians buried their dead in the sand, on their sides, with their knees curled into their chest, facing the setting sun in the direction their spirits were headed. The hot, dry desert sucked the body fluids away. The skin hardened into a leathery shell, keeping everything in place. Ironically, concern for the corpse was what created problems. To keep sand from getting into the dead person's eyes and mouth, the Egyptians began to put a basket over the body's head. Then, a basket on the head didn't seem good enough. Trays were woven for above and below the corpse to keep sand off the whole body. Soon, brick-lined pits were being built for the dead. The problem was that without the sand to wick

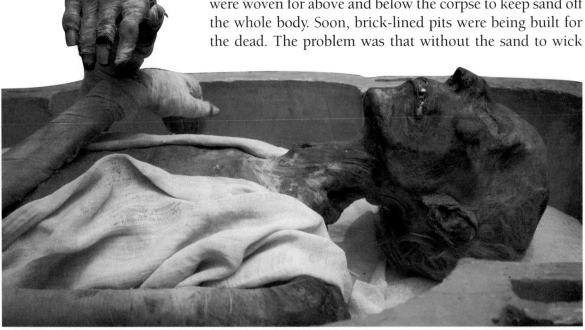

Ramesses II was publicly unwrapped in June 1886 in less than 15 minutes. His exposed body became contaminated by fungi and bacteria, which literally ate him bit by bit. In 1975 scientists used gamma rays to sterilize Ramesses II's body, and he is now stored in an anti-bacterial case.

away the moisture, the bodies were rotting. That would never do. Without the entire body, the spirits could not lounge in the Field of Reeds. Haunting was happening. And so the Egyptians experimented and gradually developed the process of **mummification** during the Old Kingdom period.

Because everyone wanted their loved ones preserved, the funeral trade was a good one. The embalmers, who prepared the dead for burial, guarded their money-making secrets, passing their skills down from father to son. What we know about making a mummy comes from the Greek historians Herodotus, who wrote during the 5th century BCE, and Diodorus Siculus, who wrote during the 1st century BCE. The Greeks were fascinated by Egypt, as they were with many foreign cultures, and wrote about both the country and its history. Herodotus and Diodorus Siculus describe three mummy options: one for the very rich, one for the not so rich, and one for the poor. From their writings, we have the following recipe for a mummy (in this case, a top-of-the-line mummy):

1. First stop for the dead is the Place of Washing, which the Egyptians called *Ibu*. After a good washing, the embalmers performed a ceremony with Nile water and a kind of salt found in the waters of the Nile called natron. The ceremony symbolizes rebirth. For more reasons than one—secrecy and stench, to name two—*Ibu* is not close to town.

2. Next stop is *Per-nefer,* the House of Mummification. Herodotus reports what went on there: "They take first a crooked piece of iron, and with it draw out the brain through the nostrils." Then the embalmers flush out the skull with water and lay it on its side to drain while they "cut along the flank . . . and take out the whole contents of the abdomen." The heart is left inside the body because the Egyptians believe this to be the most important organ. A few things are tossed because they are considered so unimportant— the brain, for one. The rest of the internal organs are

mummiya = "pitch"
When mummies were first examined, people assumed that the bodies had been dipped in pitch, which comes from tar. The fact that the mummies burned like torches when set on fire supported their incorrect assumption.

RIP AND RUN

From Diodorus Siculus we know that the embalmer who made the "cut in the flank" was called the Ripper. The Egyptians considered any cut an offense to the body. So in a symbolic performance after the cut was made, the rest of the embalmers threw stones at the Ripper and chased him away with curses.

Herodotus, *Histories,* about 450 BCE

The crouching figure of Anubis on the handle of this knife is the clue that leads scholars to believe that embalmers used this instrument to cut open corpses.

MEANWHILE
IN THE
AMERICAS...

In coastal Chile the Chinchorro people were also making mummies, but their process involved taking the body apart and then putting it back together again. They beheaded, dismembered, and skinned the corpse. Once dry, the parts were reassembled using sticks and grass stuffing to shape the body.

cleaned and stored in jars so that the spirits have a complete home when the time comes to reoccupy the body. Fingernails and toenails are wrapped with twine to keep them from falling off when the skin shrinks. The body is stuffed, covered with natron, which is even better than sand for drying, and left to dry for 40 days.

3. Next stop *Wabet*, the House of Purification. Here the embalmers remove the stuffing from the body cavity and repack it with sawdust, rags, natron, or sometimes even plants. They rub the skin with oils to restore its softness. Once the body looks its best, the wrapping begins. It can take two weeks to wrap a body and nearly 500 square yards of linen. The family of the deceased spends the next 40 days while the body is drying collecting anything that can be torn into strips to supply the embalmers with wrappings. To help the Ka and Ba recognize their body under all those rags, an artist paints a mummy mask that looks like the dead person's face.

From start to finish, embalmers chanted spells and performed rituals. The whole process took on average 70 days—unless, of course, you went for the economy option, and then the embalmers had you in and out in 7 days. And that's a wrap.

These three nesting coffins are person-shaped, or anthropoid. Only the very wealthy could afford to pay artists to carve mummy cases. The richer you were, the fancier your burial would be.

CHAPTER 7

TOMB BUILDERS
THE PYRAMID AGE /
THE OLD KINGDOM

What if you were an Egyptian tomb builder? Life for you 4,500 years ago may have gone this way:

The barge floated upstream, bumping to a stop at the dock alongside a small farming village located a week's journey south of the capital of **Mennefer**. The king's men disembarked and marched double file over the pier heading for the village center. Word of their arrival rippled from house to mud-brick house. Men and women trickled out of their homes and formed a loose ring around the king's messengers. Curious and shy, the youngest children peeked out from behind their mothers' legs. One of the king's men—a scribe—unrolled a scroll and held it at arm's length. He shouted out names. You caught your breath. Would you be on the list?

Your grandfather set the first stones in King Khufu's *mer*. Now 20 years later, the eternal home is nearly finished, but there is still much work to be done. A king's eternal home is more than just a *mer*. There are temples and causeways and walls and the queen's tombs to be built. A papyrus inscription, called the Turin Papyrus, written long after you had traveled to the afterlife, and long after kings had stopped being buried at Giza, claims the Great Pyramid was built in less than 23 years. But for all the years you can remember, you have watched your friends board the king's barge when the harvest was done. When the floods receded, and they came back, the women fussed over them, and the men treated them with respect. You caught them sometimes walking with a swagger. They had seen the world.

Not everyone came home. Those that came back brought news of the ones that stayed. They had married and had children and learned trades other than farming. They chose to stay on at the Giza Plateau and work for the king.

mennefer = "eternal beauty" During the reign of King Khufu (the Greeks called him Cheops), Mennefer was the capital city. We know it as Memphis, near modern-day Cairo.

LET THEM EAT MER

The Egyptians called the pyramids *mer*, a word whose etymology and significance is debated. Our word "pyramid" comes from the Greek word *pyramis*, a type of wheat cake shaped like a pyramid.

King Khufu's pyramid is the farthest to the right. Of the Seven Wonders of the Ancient World, it is the oldest and only one surviving. An Arab proverb best captures the pyramids' endurance: "Man fears Time, yet Time fears the pyramids."

For two weeks now you have felt the restlessness of the flood time. If the king's men call your name, will you be one who never returns? Will this be the last time you see your village and your family?

When the scribe shouts out your name, you are afraid you heard wrong. Your knees feel a little weak. You've never left your village before. What will the world be like in the north across the Nile from the capital?

You rush home to pack your things. While piling your clothing in a square and tying it into a bundle, you suddenly feel too old for your mother's kisses. She's weeping behind you. But when you turn you see the pride in her eyes. Maybe she is thinking that if you help build the king's pathway to the heavens you will get to journey to the afterlife, too.

The barge is waiting by the dock. You and several others from the village hurry to board. The boat is already loaded with young men from villages even farther south. As the river currents carry you swiftly northward, you watch your village grow smaller and smaller until you aren't sure if you can see it. The ship is noisy with bragging men who have worked many flood seasons at Giza. Their voices fade, because suddenly you wish you were back in your village, watching your mother weave reed sandals, and not on a barge among men you don't know.

What was it like for young people who worked on the pyramids of King Khufu and the pyramids of his sons? To come from small farming villages, float up the Nile to the Giza Plateau and live in a barracks town of thousands? As they approached Giza, the Great Pyramid must have appeared to thrust out of the plateau as if it would pierce the sky. The monument was so massive that it took more than 4,000 years for humans to build anything taller. Until the Eiffel Tower was built in Paris in 1889, the Great Pyramid was the tallest building on earth. What would it have felt like to a simple Egyptian peasant to be part of such a huge project? How would you have felt that first day at Giza?

Your transport barge snakes its way up one of the heavily trafficked canals that connects the Nile to the Mouth of the Lake, a delivery area near the pyramid complex. Barges loaded with stone and wood for building choke the canals, alongside barges loaded with food and supplies for the gangs of workmen, gangs of a thousand men with names like those found in a later pyramid—"Friends of Menkaure" and "Drunkards of Menkaure." Is it the vastness of the construction project that makes you stagger? Or is it the people? So many people! Thousands!

The clang of copper hammers trimming limestone and inscribing stone makes your head ache. On the south side of the pyramid, men are pounding wood wedges into the rock walls of the quarry and then soaking the wood with water. The wood expands and the rock splits.

Watch out! You are jostled by two men hustling past with clay jars slopping water. They slosh it onto mud-covered wooden tracks. Eight men push a block of limestone so large you can't imagine it moving, yet it glides over the slick, wet mud as if the stone were hollow and filled with

66 Graffiti inside Menkaure's pyramid, Giza, about 2532–2504 BCE

PYRAMID MATH

Napoleon calculated that if King Khufu and his two sons' pyramids were taken apart and used to build a protective wall, it would stand ten feet high, one foot thick, and go the entire way around France.

If the Great Pyramid were chopped into 12-inch cubes there would be enough cubes to circle the moon almost three times.

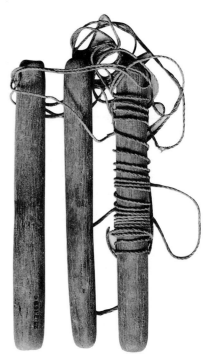

It is hard to believe that with simple tools such as this one, masons carved the building blocks for the pyramids that fit together so snuggly that a razor blade would not fit between them. This tool was used to "dress" the limestone, or make it perfectly flat.

feathers. Above you, on the wide, wedge-shaped ramp built out of broken bits of stone and rubble, there are more groups of men pushing two-and-a-half-ton blocks with the same ease as the men by your side. Still more crews at the top of the ramp are positioning the stones by lifting them into place with ropes and levers. When it is done, 2,300,000 blocks will have been hauled into place. Some of the stones inside the pyramid are granite cubes weighing as much as 40 tons.

You try to imagine what it had looked like that first season your grandfather worked here. Then it was nothing more than an empty plateau. You remember his stories of how they chose where to place the very first stones. The priests had tracked the movement of the stars in the Great Bear constellation across the night sky. Using the stars for bearings and applying "the instrument of knowing," a simple handheld rod with a string that dropped straight to the ground, they had staked out the base. Then, in a symbolic ceremony, King Khufu himself had pointed out true north by lining up the headdress of a priestess with the star that was the hoof of the Great Bear. The calculations were so precise that thousands of years later modern scholars would discover the Great Pyramid was less than a tenth of a degree off true north.

The orientation was critical for the king's entrance to the afterlife. The pyramid represented his rampway to heaven. From the Pyramid Texts we learn that the pyramid was the "stairway in order to reach the heights...stairs to the sky, which are laid down for the king, that he may ascend thereon to the heavens." And your grandfather was there to see the first rock put in place.

When you arrive at the barracks, the smell of fresh baking bread makes your mouth water. Bakers pull loaves out of ovens large enough for you to stand in. You take some bread for yourself and then some for your grandfather's Ka. You wander to the west side of the pyramid looking for his tomb. Your mother told you that his tomb is a miniature version of King Khufu's *mer*, except grandfather's is made from mud brick instead of stone. You pass the tomb of a husband and wife who worked on the Great Pyramid. You are one of the few who can read bits and pieces of hieroglyphs. What you read makes you quicken your pace past

📖 Pyramid Texts, about 2375–2184 BCE

Egyptians built tombs with many secret passageways in hopes of foiling tomb robbers. This wall painting shows a sarcophagus being taken into the depths of the tomb, while the gods wait for the deceased to arrive in the kingdom of the Underworld.

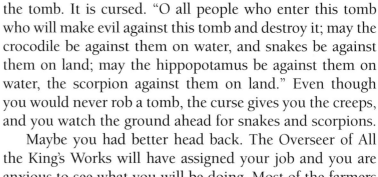

Graffiti inside Menkaure's pyramid, Giza, about 2532–2504 BCE

Written all over the walls inside King Unas's pyramid are the oldest surviving inscriptions of the Pyramid Texts. The Pyramid Texts guide the deceased on the treacherous journey through the Underworld.

the tomb. It is cursed. "O all people who enter this tomb who will make evil against this tomb and destroy it; may the crocodile be against them on water, and snakes be against them on land; may the hippopotamus be against them on water, the scorpion against them on land." Even though you would never rob a tomb, the curse gives you the creeps, and you watch the ground ahead for snakes and scorpions.

Maybe you had better head back. The Overseer of All the King's Works will have assigned your job and you are anxious to see what you will be doing. Most of the farmers have to do all the heavy lifting, but maybe you will be lucky since you can read a little. Maybe you will be assigned a more skilled job. You hope that you can work on one of the boats in one of the boat pits. Wouldn't it be fabulous to be a boat builder for the afterlife? To help build the boat that King Khufu will use to navigate the stars?

One day, maybe your children will work at Giza on King Khufu's children's pyramids. Maybe when your grandchildren row into the Mouth of the Lake they will tremble at the sight of the Great Sphinx. The statue has the body of a lion and the head of man. The Great Sphinx guards the Giza Plateau. It faces east with its face tilted slightly back to catch the first rays of the rising sun. It was built by the Pharaoh Khafre (Chephren), the son of King Khufu; he also built the second of the three pyramids at Giza.

In modern times the Sphinx still has the power to make one tremble even though its face is battered and its body scored from

Scholars believe that the Great Sphinx—silent guardian of the Giza pyramids—is the largest stone sculpture ever made by man. Today, the Great Sphinx is getting smaller, crumbling from the effects of wind, humidity, and Cairo's smog.

erosion. From its tail curled around its right haunch to the tip of its paws, the Sphinx would stretch out over most of a football field. It's tall enough to see over the top of a six-story building. The braided beard that once hung from the Sphinx's chin fell long ago and smashed into bits. A scrap of faded color near one ear is all that's left of its once bright paint. All of the Sphinx would have crumbled if it hadn't spent most of its life protectively buried in sand that had blown around it.

The Sphinx was up to its neck in sand 3,400 years ago. According to the inscriptions on a stone tablet known as the Dream Stela, which sits between the Sphinx's paws, Prince Thutmose "came traveling at the time of midday. He rested in the shadow of the great god." In a dream, the Sphinx whispered in the prince's ear promising him, "I shall give you the kingship," if the prince would just clear away the sand. Some say that the prince made the whole story up to get away with murder. He was not next in line for the throne. His brother should have been king. Prince Thutmose had his brother killed and became King Thutmose IV. The Egyptians might have driven a murderer off the throne, but who was going to argue with the word of the Sphinx? If you had been there, would you?

❝ Dream Stela, about 1419–1386 BCE

MODERN TALES

Urban legend has it that Napoleon's soldiers used the Sphinx's nose for target practice and shot it off. But the nose was missing long before Napoleon came along. In a fit of religious fervor against "graven images," an offended Muslim knocked it off several hundred years earlier.

CHAPTER 8

FROM MONARCHY TO ANARCHY AND BACK AGAIN

THE FIRST INTERMEDIATE PERIOD AND THE MIDDLE KINGDOM

SEEING DOUBLE

Before the unification Egypt had two capitals—Memphis in the north and Abydos in the south. Memphis was the capital city during the Old Kingdom. During the First Intermediate Period, Hieracleopolis was the capital city, then Thebes.

❝ *Admonitions of Ipuwer*, 1991–1782 BCE

❝ Ankhtyfy's tomb inscriptions, near Luxor, about 2100 BCE

The First Intermediate Period began with blood. With each passing year of Pepi II's reign, which began in 2278 BCE, the aging king's power slipped a little more. The governors of the outlying provinces who all had once lived in the capital city with Pepi II moved out to the rural lands they governed. Until then, whatever each province produced, such as grain, had gone to the capital to be handed out by the great and powerful King Pepi II. Now goods remained in the province to be distributed by the governor. Power shifted. It shifted, bit by bit, from the capital to the provinces—from the king to the governors.

The governors, accustomed to palace life, began to build their own luxurious houses. They financed their rich lifestyle by keeping more and more of the local goods. Soon they needed artists to decorate their homes and their tombs. Rural Egypt changed. Wealth and culture shifted, bit by bit, from the capital to the provinces—from the control of the king to the control of the governors.

A papyrus known as the *Admonitions of Ipuwer* tells how wealth moved from royalty to ragamuffin: "poor men have become owners of wealth, and he who could not make sandals for himself is now a possessor of riches...noblemen are in distress while the poor man is full of joy...the land turns around as does a potter's wheel."

One typical governor, Ankhtyfy, ruled two provinces. Inscribed on the pillars of his tomb are the details of his life. He begins his autobiography by bragging, "I was the beginning and the end of mankind, since nobody like myself existed before, nor will he exist...I surpassed the feats of the ancestors, and coming generations will not be able to equal me...." This man did not suffer from low self-esteem.

It was also common for governors to brag that they could support the people in their community while the rest of Egypt starved. Ankhtyfy apparently was just as conceited as all the others because his inscription says,

> I gave bread to the hungry and clothing to the naked... I gave sandals to the barefooted. The whole country has become like locusts going upstream and downstream in search of food; but never did I allow anybody in need to go from this province to another one. I am the hero without equal.

Ankhtyfy's tomb inscriptions, near Luxor, about 2100 BCE

Boasts like these led scholars to believe that the First Intermediate Period and all its chaos were brought about by famine. Was all of Egypt starving? Is that why the country fell apart? Archaeologists who study ancient climates don't think that is true. There were droughts in the Old Kingdom and the king was still able to maintain control. And there were good harvests during the First Intermediate Period and yet chaos ruled. The boasts about feeding the hungry were most likely meant to send the message to the people that they needed the governor, that without their local ruler they would suffer as the rest of the country was supposedly suffering.

With a goose in every pot—on his tomb walls, at least—Ankhtyfy makes the bold claim that he alone saved Egypt from famine. Although boasts like these were common on tomb walls, stories of cannibalism were not. Ankhtyfy's tomb inscriptions mention cannibalism as one not-so-pleasant solution to famine.

A woman balances food and goods on her head during a time of plenty. When flood levels were just right, harvests were bountiful and trade was vigorous.

Governors had always recruited military troops from their provinces for their king. Now instead of sending soldiers to the capital, they were using the troops for their own scrambles for power. The strong grew stronger, and the wealthy grew wealthier. The central government splintered. The king's power slipped further.

When the last pharaoh of the Old Kingdom, Pepi II, finally died in his 90s, Egypt was a country divided into feeble kingdoms festering from civil wars. The First Intermediate Period was bathed in blood. The Greek historian Herodotus writes about a First Intermediate queen, royal murders, and revenge. Determined to avenge her brother's death, the queen "devised a cunning scheme.... She constructed a spacious underground chamber.... Inviting to a banquet those Egyptians whom she knew to have had a chief share in the murder of her brother, she suddenly, as they were feasting, let the river in upon them, by means of a secret duct of large size." The scheming murderers drowned while the queen (a scheming murderess herself) escaped through a secret passageway.

The kings who followed Pepi II never lasted long. None during the First Intermediate Period had the strength to pull Egypt back together again. Egypt entered a dark age. Later, literature would paint a bleak picture of this trough between two times of glory. Texts written in the Middle Kingdom about the chaos and misery have depressing titles,

Herodotus, *Histories*, about 450 BCE

such as *Dialogue Between a Man Tired of Life and His Ba*. The stories were sometimes as gloomy as the titles. In the *Dialogue* the miserable character claims, "my name reeks, more than the smell of bird-droppings on summer days." He writes that "Mercy has perished" and that "hearts are selfish, and every man is stealing his fellow's belongings." Later Middle Kingdom literature moans the loss of order during the First Intermediate Period; it groans at the unrest. It claims the Nile itself stopped flowing, and the sun lost its brilliance.

But the writings that actually come from the First Intermediate Period aren't quite so negative. Some stories are about problems, but problems that could be overcome. Problems wrestled with. Problems solved. Not everything was bleak for everyone. With the decline of the king's power, people suddenly began to think for themselves. If the king could not control Egypt, was he really a god? Perhaps, if the king was not perfect and he could enter the afterlife, others could, too.

Directions to the next world, which previously had been available only to the king, were now being written on the inside and outside of coffins. Maps of the underworld were drawn, too, so that the dead could find their way. Just to be on the safe side, artists drew eyes on the outside of the coffin so that the dead inside could read what was written outside. The Coffin Texts became available to the upper levels of society who could afford a burial.

Without the rigid formulas of the old ways, new ways were possible. The paintings and stories in Ankhtyfy's tomb are examples of this new freedom. They are unlike anything from the Old Kingdom. The artists painted in bold new styles. They painted scenes of everyday activities such as spinning and weaving, with craftspeople using new inventions. Artistry and technology bloomed when the artisans were no longer told how things must be done.

Scholars do not agree on exactly when the First Intermediate Period ended and the Middle Kingdom began. The list of kings is confusing, and dates overlap. But one thing is certain: when the Middle Kingdom was in full swing, centralized power was back.

66 *Dialogue Between a Man Tired of Life and His Ba*, about 2940–1782 BCE

THE GODS GET EVEN

Kings from the First Intermediate Period were not known for their kindness. Manetho, an Egyptian priest and historian, writes about one particularly cruel king in the 9th dynasty. The gods, Manetho claims, got even. They drove the king insane, and then had him eaten by a crocodile.

Archaeologist Flinders Petrie and his wife, Hilda, study the excavation site at Kahun. The locals affectionately called Flinders Petrie the Father of Pots because of his obsession for mapping the location of every single shard.

Archaeologists who have been digging and surveying at the pyramid town of Kahun on and off since 1889 have discovered what urban life was like in the Middle Kingdom. The walled village built beside the pyramid complex was home to the king's workers and their families. Judging from the size of their grain silos, there was enough food to support as many as 5,000 people. Seeds found in the ancient layers show botanists what the vegetation looked like back then. Poppies, lupines, and jasmine bloomed and perfumed the air. Gardeners tended their peas, beans, radishes, and cucumbers.

Nearby, archaeologists piece together life in the royal court as the area is excavated. One papyrus, *The Tale of Sinuhe*, gives us an idea of how a Middle Kingdom palace functioned. It was divided into three main parts. The royal family and their servants lived in an area called the Nursery. Banquets were held in the Pillared Hall. And business was conducted in the Audience Hall.

The story of the royal guard Sinuhe reveals that even in the Middle Kingdom plots to murder the king and overthrow the throne were a constant worry. King Amenemhet had united the country, but not all those governors were

willing to give up their power now that they had tasted it. Prince Senwosert was on his way home from battle when messengers brought news from the palace that his father had been murdered. The story goes that Sinuhe, overhearing their message, panicked and fled Egypt. Crossing the desert, he thought he had met his end: "Thirst's attack overtook me, and I was scorched, my throat parched. I said, 'This is the taste of death.'"

But just when he was sure he was a goner, Sinuhe was rescued by a tribe of nomads. The head of the tribe tells Sinuhe, "stay with me; I shall do you good." True to his word, the headsman made Sinuhe a wealthy and important man. But when Sinuhe grew old he began to miss his beloved homeland. Sinuhe wanted to be buried in Egypt. He wanted to build his tomb—his resting place for eternity—in his own country. Sinuhe writes to Senwosert, now king of Egypt; "Whatever God fated this flight—be gracious, and bring me home! Surely You will let me see the place where my heart still stays! What matters more than my being buried in the land where I was born?" King Senwosert answers, "Return to Egypt! And you will see the Residence where you grew up."

Back in Egypt, the king gave Sinuhe a home and food and fine linen. All his needs were taken care of: "A pyramid of stone was built for me...the masons who construct the pyramid measured out its foundations; the draughtsman drew in it; the overseer of sculptors carved in it." Sinuhe's tale, like Egypt itself, was in for a happy ending. Using "landing" as a metaphor for death—an appropriate word choice for a tale of journey—Sinuhe ends his story by saying, "I was in the favors of the king's giving, until the day of landing came." And now Egypt was in the favors of the king, too. It had traveled from monarchy to anarchy and back again.

The Tale of Sinuhe, about 1991–1926 BCE

The Tale of Sinuhe, about 1991–1926 BCE

The Tale of Sinuhe, about 1991–1926 BCE

FAIR-Y TALE

The Tale of Sinuhe was handed down through the generations, told again and again. Teachers told the tale in their classrooms, too. The moral of the story—that Egypt was the finest country in the world—made it a favorite among the Egyptians.

CHAPTER 9

❝ HOMER,
DIODORUS SICULUS,
HERODOTUS,
EBERS PAPYRUS,
TOMB PAINTINGS
AND ENGRAVINGS,
AND EDWIN
SMITH PAPYRUS

TAKE TWO MICE AND CALL ME IN THE MORNING

MEDICINE AND MAGIC

❝ Homer, *Odyssey*, about
725 BCE

If you became sick in ancient times, Egypt was where you would want to be. It offered the best medical care. The Greek poet Homer writes in about 725 BCE in the *Odyssey* about Egyptian doctors, "In medical knowledge the Egyptian leaves the rest of the world behind." Egyptians began practicing medicine by applying salves to the eyes as long as 6,000 years ago, and over the millennia their skills became world renowned, so much so that rulers of other countries

Carved into the wall of a temple dedicated to learning are 37 surgical tools, many similar to modern instruments—scalpels, forceps, probes, hooks, and sponges. Although the ancient Egyptians didn't perform internal surgeries as we do today, they did treat complicated wounds successfully.

sent for Egyptian doctors to cure their ills. Their treatments may sound primitive to us, but no doubt 6,000 years from now our "modern medicine" will seem positively barbaric to future scientists.

In many ways, medicine in ancient Egypt was like medicine today. Doctors then studied for many years in medical schools called *peru-ankh*, or "houses of life." They studied textbooks to learn how to recognize diseases by their symptoms and what to do to cure the patient. The Greek historian Diodorus Siculus writes, "They administer their treatments in accordance with a written law which was composed in ancient times by many famous physicians."

The Ebers Papyrus is one of the oldest medical documents from anywhere in the ancient world. The papyrus scroll is more than 60 feet long and is inscribed on both sides. Some of the cures don't sound too bad. For indigestion the Ebers Papyrus advises patients to "crush a hog's tooth and put it inside four sugar cakes. Eat for four days." But other cures sound pretty disgusting. For a cut, "after the scab has fallen off put on it: Scribe's excrement. Mix in fresh milk and apply as a poultice."

Considering that 19 types of excrement are mentioned in the cures, from fly excrement to ostrich excrement, it's no surprise Egyptian doctors had a problem with disgruntled patients. They handled malpractice efficiently, though. Diordorus writes,

> If they follow the rules of this law as they read them in the sacred book and yet are unable to save their patient, they are absolved from any charge; but if they go contrary to the law's prescriptions they must submit to a trial with death as the penalty.

If you're a physician and you follow the rules, all's well. But get creative with your treatments and you won't be treating anyone, unless it's in the afterlife.

Just as medical doctors do today, in ancient Egypt doctors specialized. The Greek historian Herodotus writes, "The practice of medicine is so divided among them that each physician treats one disease and no more. There are plenty

per + *ankh* = "house" + "life" We might call the Egyptians' House of Life a library. Although sometimes a separate building, it was more often the room (or area) in a temple where all the records and texts were kept and where people could study them.

Diodorus Siculus, *Biblioteca Historica*, about 90–21 BCE

Ebers Papyrus, about 1550 BCE

Diodorus Siculus, *Biblioteca Historica*, about 90–21 BCE

Herodotus, *Histories*, about 450 BCE

of physicians everywhere. Some are eye-doctors, some deal with the head, others with the teeth or the belly, and some with hidden maladies. . . ." The Ebers Papyrus even had a section on psychiatry, directing doctors on how to diagnose and treat depression.

The Egyptians had a cure for the common cold that was probably as good as anything you can find in a pharmacy today. It required a dose of the milk of a mother who had given birth to a boy, while chanting the spell, "May you flow out . . . who causes the seven openings in the head to ache." The Egyptians understood injuries caused by an accident, or in battle. They understood parasites and worms such as tapeworms, which they called "snakes in the belly." But for germs that couldn't be seen, Egyptians believed demons were responsible. There's nothing like a good spell to rid the body of evil spirits. The Ebers Papyrus states, "Magic is effective together with medicine. Medicine is effective together with magic." And so many medical treatments were odd combinations of science and magic.

But just because doctors in ancient Egypt used magic to cure what they couldn't see, it didn't mean they weren't gifted physicians in terms of science. Brain surgery was successfully performed 5,000 years ago, broken arms set, legs amputated, and the patients survived because of the skill of the surgeons. We think that because surgical instruments were made from a volcanic glass called obsidian that the surgeries were more like hackings, but the flakes were sharper than scalpels used today. One tomb carving shows what many Egyptologists believe to be a tracheotomy, which is cutting open the throat to clear the airway so the patient can breathe. At Saqqara, in the Tomb of the Physician, wall paintings of surgery are captioned with

“ Ebers Papyrus, about 1550 BCE

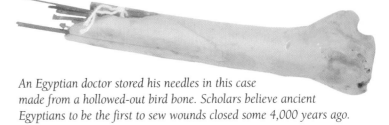

An Egyptian doctor stored his needles in this case made from a hollowed-out bird bone. Scholars believe ancient Egyptians to be the first to sew wounds closed some 4,000 years ago.

The wadjet eye, or Eye of Horus, was a popular healing and protection amulet. A variation of the wadjet eye tops the pyramid on the American dollar bill.

the words, "Do not let it be painful," which leads scholars to believe that Egyptian surgeons used anesthesia.

66 Wall paintings from the Tomb of the Physician, Saqqara, about 2300 BCE

Egyptian doctors used many herbs to heal. The ancient Egyptians believed that demons hated honey, in fact, that they feared it. Honey was used in many of the remedies to ward off evil spirits. We now know that honey boosts the immune system and is an antibiotic, as are onions, another frequently prescribed remedy. Garlic, used for almost everything, is about 1 percent the strength of penicillin, a good medicine to fight bacteria. Egyptian prescriptions worked. And just like our modern physicians, Egyptian doctors adjusted the dosage according to the age of the patient. "If it is a big child, he should swallow it like a draught, if he is still in swaddles, it should be rubbed by his nurse in milk and thereafter sucked on 4 days."

66 Ebers Papyrus, about 1550 BCE

The Egyptians even fashioned an inhaler for asthmatics, "bring seven stones and heat them on fire. Take one of them, place parts of these drugs over it, cover it with a new jar with a pierced bottom. Introduce a tube of reed through this hole and put your mouth on this tube so that you swallow its fumes." Experience taught the doctors that there were some things beyond their skill, just as there are today. When

66 Ebers Papyrus, about 1550 BCE

examining "a patient with stomach disease suffering from pain in the arms, in the breast and on one side of the stomach" doctors were advised to "say 'death threatens.'" The symptoms described what we now know is a heart attack.

So what would a doctor's visit be like for someone like you in ancient Egypt? If you were a 13-year-old girl in ancient Egypt, you would likely be married and have a child. Suppose your child had a cough. If you were wealthy the doctor would come to your home. He or she (yes, there were women doctors) would begin by taking your child's pulse. "It is there that the heart speaks. It is there that every physician and every priest of Sekhmet places his fingers...." Next the doctor would ask you questions he or she had learned from medical books. These questions would be much like the questions a doctor would ask you today—with a few exceptions. The doctor would ask, "Do you have any enemies?" and "Did you get anyone angry lately?" because they believed that sometimes the ill wishes of others brought on the demons. The doctor would then chant a spell to drive out the evil spirits causing your child's illness.

Children were breast-fed until they were three in Egypt, and doctors knew that the health of the child was affected by what the nursing mother ate. In the case of a cough, the doctor would have you eat a mouse, so that through you, your nursing child would get the mouse medicine. Then to be sure that the spell went to the right person, the doctor would make an amulet, or charm. He'd wrap the bones of the mouse in a linen cloth, tie it with seven knots, and hang it around your child's neck. Don't knock it. We have no cure for the common cold yet, either. But we have progressed in 6,000 years, haven't we? Our surgical blades may not be as sharp as Egyptian obsidian flakes. And our medications may have more bad side effects than the natural remedies that the ancients administered. But at least no one feeds you a mouse.

66 Edwin Smith Papyrus, about 1600 BCE

KERMIT IN KEMET

Spells did not *ask* help from gods; they compelled them to help. If a spell was done just right, no god could resist. The lion-headed goddess Sekhmet was believed to cause and cure plagues. The frog goddess Heket protected women during childbirth. Why a frog? Because when the Nile flooded, frogs were everywhere. The Egyptians associated frogs with birth of the new season and good fortune.

CHAPTER 10

HANDS OFF
THE SECOND INTERMEDIATE PERIOD

66 MANETHO,
PAPYRUS SALLIER I,
TOMB INSCRIPTIONS
OF AHMOSE,
AND JOSEPHUS

The invaders didn't swoop across Egypt like a tidal wave. At the beginning of the Second Intermediate Period, they trickled in—immigrants from the east settling into the delta of northern Egypt. We call the invaders the Hyksos. Soon so many Hyksos had moved into the delta that they had their own king—and that irritated the king of Egypt. This was Egyptian soil, after all. Who did that foreign king think he was ruling in Egypt? No matter how hard the Hyksos tried to blend in, they were still foreigners. It didn't matter if they worshipped Egyptian gods, wore Egyptian clothes, or ate Egyptian food. They were still foreigners. Even their Egyptian name, *heqa-khasut*, smacked of somewhere else. It meant "chiefs of foreign lands."

True, the Hyksos brought with them the hump-backed Zebu cattle that the Egyptians liked so much. And those apples sure were tasty. . . not to mention the olives. And oh,

Hyksos is a Greek word. The Egyptians called the Hyksos *heqa-khasut*. The original translation of the Egyptian by historian Josephus that is still often used ("the Shepherd Kings") is wrong; *heqa-khasut* means "chiefs of foreign lands."

Runway models show off the fashions of foreign tribes (top), which were quite different from Egyptian dress (bottom). Well, maybe not runway models.

the sound of the lyre and the lute! Their notes echoed through the chambers of the royal palace. Then there was the vertical loom. For weaving linen it couldn't be beat. The Hyksos' potter's wheels were better, too. But why were the Hyksos hiring scribes to copy Egyptian texts? Stealing Egyptian medical practices, no doubt. And it was totally unacceptable to build Avaris, a walled fortress, and claim it as their capital.

Manetho, an Egyptian priest, writes that the Hyksos' king "found a city very favorably situated on the east of the . . . Nile, and called it Avaris. This place he rebuilt and fortified with massive walls, planting there a garrison of as many as 240,000 heavy-armed men to guard his frontier."

Manetho, *Aegyptiaca*, about 300 BCE

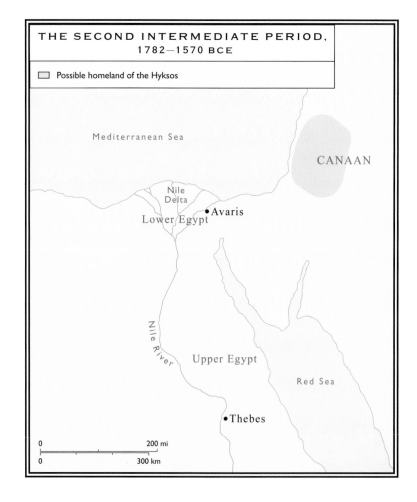

THE SECOND INTERMEDIATE PERIOD, 1782—1570 BCE

Possible homeland of the Hyksos

Mediterranean Sea

CANAAN

Nile Delta

Lower Egypt

•Avaris

Nile River

Upper Egypt

Red Sea

•Thebes

0   200 mi

0   300 km

Hippos were considered bad omens, associated with the evil god Seth. They were more dangerous than crocodiles, all too often capsizing papyrus boats traveling the Nile.

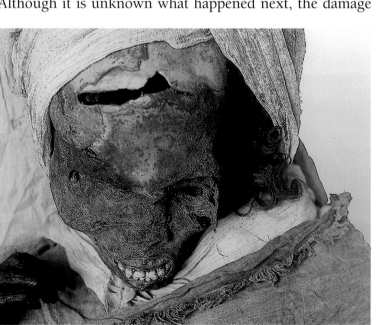

Nowhere did the Hyksos' foreignness offend Egyptians as much as at Avaris. Why, those Hyksos dared to live in the same place that they buried their dead. Barbarians!

The king of the Hyksos was like a pebble in the Egyptian king's sandal. He irritated him just by being there, but war didn't break out until the insult. The Hyksos king sent a message to the ruler of Egypt, King Seqenenre. The Hyksos king complained that King Seqenenre's hippos in the royal pools "were keeping him awake at night with their grunts." *Do* something, he demanded. Given that Avaris was hundreds of miles from Thebes, where the king and his hippos lived, this was nothing short of a slap in the face. King Seqenenre was furious. Although it is unknown what happened next, the damage

❝ Papyrus Sallier I, about 1212–1202 BCE

King Seqenenre's body took a beating on the battlefield. He suffered wounds from a mace, arrows, and an axe to the head, which killed him.

WAIT UNTIL WE'RE
GOOD AND READY

War in ancient times was
not continuous. It might
take months to prepare for
a battle and then months,
or even years, before the
next battle was fought.

BOWS

The Hyksos made their
bows from horn, sinew,
and wood.

to King Seqenenre's skull indicates it didn't turn out well for the Egyptian side. During that time kings commanded the armies and led the soldiers into battle. Archaeologists have identified King Seqenenre's head, and it's not pretty. He took a battle axe to the forehead and was stabbed in the neck after he fell to the ground. This attack was the beginning of a war that would last nearly 25 years, from about 1574 to 1550 BCE, and span the reign of three Egyptian kings.

The Egyptians were farmers, not warriors. They were peaceful people. They were not conquerors by nature. And nowhere was that more obvious than in their army. It was unorganized. The soldiers served part-time and their weapons were not much more than farm tools adapted for battle. The few full-time soldiers were trained as palace guards, border police, or trade-ship escorts—not warriors. For the occasional battle outside of Egypt, the king hired foreign mercenaries because Egyptians didn't want to die away from home. An improper burial meant wandering the desert for eternity—not a pleasant haunting.

The Hyksos army was made up of professional soldiers. They drove chariots, wore body armor and leather helmets, and wielded bows designed to shoot arrows farther than ordinary wooden bows. It's no surprise that the Hyksos beat the Egyptians in those first battles. But the Egyptians learned from the encounters. They stole the design of the chariot from the Hyksos and then improved upon it. The Egyptians made the chariot lighter. The redesign positioned the driver over the axle and they covered the wooden axle with metal so that it turned more smoothly. These changes made it easier for the horse to pull the chariot. The driver stood, holding onto straps for balance, with a soldier at his side. The soldier held a shield and was armed with a bow and arrows, a sword, and a javelin. The back of the chariot was open so that the charioteers could jump out with ease and engage in hand-to-hand combat with the enemy.

The Egyptians trained. They held battle competitions in front of the king. Archers shot at targets. Wrestlers grappled with one another. Swordsmen clashed blades. What had once been a rag-tag scrabble of men became an organized military. But they still had work to do on their style of waging war. Before a battle, the Egyptians notified the enemy which day they planned to attack and where. If the enemy wasn't ready, the Egyptians rescheduled. And if the enemy retreated into their fortress, rather than rudely barging in, the Egyptians would patiently wait outside hoping to starve them out. Unfortunately, Egypt's enemies weren't always as courteous.

Much of what we know about the war with the Hyksos comes from the tomb of an Egyptian officer. Ahmose, son of Ibana, inscribed on the columns and walls of his tomb details of the many battles he fought with the Hyksos. "I was taken to the ship *Northern*, because I was brave. I followed the king on foot when he rode about on his chariot. When the town of Avaris was besieged, I fought bravely on

SHORT PEOPLE

Despite his stature as a military man, Ahmose, son of Ibana, was only five feet tall. Today that would be considered short, but in ancient Egypt it was an average height.

❝ Tomb inscriptions of Ahmose of Ibana, El-Kab, about 1550 BCE

This "modern" six-spoke chariot wheel replaced the earlier, less stable four-spoke version. The wheels were attached to the hub with wet cow intestines. When the intestines dried, they shrank and hardened, creating a strong connection.

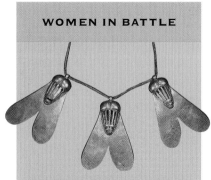

WOMEN IN BATTLE

The king of Egypt's mother, Queen Ahhotep I, received at least three Golden Fly medals for her brave part in battles against the Hyksos. She lived more than 90 years. She and her medals were buried beside her son.

 Josephus quoting passages concerning the Hyksos from Manetho's *Aegyptiaca*, about 37–100 CE

foot in his majesty's presence." Ahmose was rewarded for his valor, he "was appointed to the ship *Rising in Memphis.* Then there was fighting on the water…I made a seizure and carried off a hand." To keep track of the number of enemy soldiers killed, it was the custom to cut off a hand and present it to the king.

For his victories—and the hands that went with them—Ahmose, son of Ibana, was awarded seven times the medal of honor called the Golden Fly. The Golden Fly was a gilded pin shaped like a horsefly. Although the horsefly may seem like an odd shape for a war medal, the Egyptians chose it because the horsefly was the tormentor of beasts. This medal of honor was presented only to the bravest soldiers.

A Roman historian writing in the first century CE, Josephus, tells us how it turned out in the end for the Hyksos:

> They enclosed Avaris with a high strong wall in order to safeguard all their possessions and spoils. The Egyptian king attempted by siege to force them to surrender, blockading the fortress with an army of 480,000 men. Finally, giving up the siege in despair, he concluded a treaty by which they should all depart from Egypt.

Archaeologists working at Avaris don't see evidence of a mass slaughter. They believe the Hyksos were expelled and took their possessions with them. One way or the other the message was the same: Hands off Egypt.

CHAPTER 11

A TALE OF TWO DEITIES
HATSHEPSUT AND THUTMOSE III

❝ GOVERNMENT RECORDS, HATSHEPSUT'S TOMB INSCRIPTIONS, TOMB INSCRIPTION OF AN ARMY SCRIBE, AND INSCRIPTIONS AT KARNAK

When families get together for holidays and special occasions—after the latest news has been exchanged, and a good meal eaten, and the day has grown long—the old stories come out. Each story is told as if it were the first time, even though everyone has heard it a hundred times before, and can anticipate the next line before it is said out loud. Why are these worn family histories shared again and again? Partly because they hold the character of the people who are in them—they can show us grandma's fierce independence, grandpa's stubborn streak, cousin's temper, and great aunt's love of animals. They hold a hint of who we are and how we hope to be remembered (and some things that we wish had been forgotten). It is the same with the ancient Egyptian stories told on tomb and temple walls and the tales that circle the columns in the colonnades. Through the millennia, the stories pass down to us keys to unlock the mystery of the people who lived so long ago.

Queen Hatshepsut's terraced mortuary temple was carved out of the rock cliffs at Deir el-Bahri. Hidden in a secret tomb south of her temple were the coffins of some of the greatest kings from the New Kingdom, including Amenhotep I, Thutmose I, II and III, Sety I, and Ramesses I and II.

Nearly 3,500 years ago Queen Hatshepsut—or as she would have called herself, *King* Hatshepsut—chose the stories she wanted remembered. Some are true, and others she made up to justify a woman ruling Egypt. How does a queen become a king? How does a king transform into a god? Sometimes it's all in the story you choose to tell.

66 Ineni, government records, about 1500 BCE

When King Thutmose II died in 1504 BCE, his son, Thutmose III, was too young to rule Egypt. Although his exact age is unknown, it is possible that he was just a young child. So, as was custom, the widowed queen took over until the young king was old enough to rule by himself. The records tell us: "Having ascended into heaven Thutmose II became united with the gods.... Hatshepsut governed Egypt, and the Two Lands were under her control. People worked for her, and Egypt bowed her head."

As a queen, Hatshepsut's powers were limited. When a king took the throne, he became a god and the middleman (or middlegod?) between the heavenly gods and the people. One of his most important jobs was to please the gods. That guaranteed the desired balance known as *ma'at*. Egypt could then flourish. No king meant no *ma'at*, which meant no flourishing. Egyptians would be doomed to the chaos of the Intermediate Periods. If Hatshepsut hoped to maintain *ma'at*, she must first become a king. She needed to show the people that the gods were pleased with her as the ruler, that the gods recognized her as king, and that she herself was indeed divine. What better way to prove her divinity than to claim that it was the gods' idea in the first place? Who would question a choice made by the gods?

Hatshepsut set out to show Egypt that she was no mere mortal, but the daughter of the great god Amun, who personally chose her to be king. To justify her kingship, Hatshepsut made up a story of her birth and commissioned

Thutmose III wears royal accessories. The headcloth was usually made from striped cloth, pulled tightly across the forehead and tied behind the head with two flaps hanging over the shoulders. A cobra on the brow protected the king. A formal fake beard is fastened with loops around the ears.

artists to illustrate it. In the final scene Hatshepsut is presented to all the gods, who recognize her as king. To be sure there was no doubt about her destiny, Hatshepsut included in the text these words, supposedly from Amun himself, "This daughter of mine . . . I have appointed successor upon my throne. . . . It is she who will lead you. Obey her words and unite yourselves at her command."

⟦❝⟧ Inscription at Hatshepsut's mortuary temple, Deir el-Bahari, about 1500 BCE

In just seven years Hatshepsut transformed herself from a dutiful co-ruler into a deity. She wore a king's crown and clothing. She carried the king's staff. She even hung the king's ceremonial hairpiece, a braided beard, from her ears with string.

But perhaps the story that Hatshepsut would most want us to know is about the trade expedition to Punt. The story is drawn in detail on the walls of the temple where she was worshipped after death. The story shows how Hatshepsut added to Egypt's wealth by focusing her reign on trade and exploration. It shows that with Hatshepsut as king, there was a whole lot of flourishing going on in Egypt. There was *ma'at*. A series of pictures and captions tell the story of the journey to Punt.

Five sailing ships manned with soldiers, officials, and rowers leave Egypt. When they arrive off foreign shores they anchor and all climb into small boats loaded with trinkets for trade. While making their way through the jungle of ebony and palm trees, the Egyptian traders come across a village. Beehive-shaped huts made from woven palm fronds sit up on stilts so far above the ground that the only way to get inside is to climb ladders leading from the ground up to the doorways.

The great god Amun sits supportively behind King Hatshepsut. She chooses to be shown as a man in king's clothing (with Amun's approval) to make it clear to everyone that she is in charge.

Egyptian sailors familiar with travel along the Nile were unaccustomed to the dangers of the open sea. The long trip to the mysterious land of Punt would be similar to today's adventurers taking off for the moon. Hey, you up front—look where you're going!

The exact location of Punt is not known, but the animals in the scenes are clearly African. There are leopards, rhinoceros, and giraffes. The carvings show trees full of monkeys. Scholars believe that the expedition took place in the spring because the birds in the pictures are nesting.

The village chief greets the Egyptian traders with the question: "How have you arrived at this land unknown to the men of Egypt? Have you come down from the roads of the Heavens?" The chief's wife and children accompany him. The Egyptians give the natives gifts of beads and bracelets. The native guides lead the Egyptian traders into the heart of Punt, where they all work together collecting ebony and incense to bring home to Hatshepsut. Hatshepsut brags on her temple walls about all the wonderful things Egypt will enjoy because of her leadership:

The loading of the ships very heavily with marvels of the country of Punt; all goodly fragrant woods... with ebony and pure ivory, with...eye-cosmetics, with apes, monkeys, dogs and with skins of the

💬 Inscription at Hatshepsut's mortuary temple, Deir el-Bahari, about 1500 BCE

💬 Inscription at Hatshepsut's mortuary temple, Deir el-Bahari, about 1500 BCE

southern panther, with natives and their children. Never was brought the like of this for any king who has been since the beginning.

Once back in Egypt the sailors unload. They wrestle with full-grown trees that have been transplanted into baskets and slung over poles for transport. Others shoulder pots and some herd animals. Hatshepsut accepts it all as her due, in the name of Egypt and her godly father Amun. A small figure in the background of one of the last scenes offers incense to the great god Amun. It is Thutmose III. But Thutmose III would not stay in the background forever. His turn on the throne was coming.

Just as Hatshepsut had a favorite story that showed us the character of her time in power, so did Thutmose III. His was the battle of Megiddo. Thutmose III's military victories were inscribed on the inner walls of the sanctuary at Karnak. The stories come from the journal entries of an army scribe. The scribe tells us, "I recorded the victories the king won in every land, putting them in writing according to the facts."

While waiting to come of age and take his rightful place as the king of Egypt, Thutmose III trained with the army. When Hatshepsut's 22-year reign ended in 1483 BCE he came to the throne a skilled and daring general. His military abilities were put to the test immediately. Expecting Egypt to be weak with a new and unproven king in charge, rebels took control of the city of Megiddo. Whoever controlled Megiddo controlled one of the most important trade routes in the world. Megiddo is located in what is today called the Jezreel Valley in modern Israel. The city, towering nearly a hundred feet above the valley, controlled

MISSING MUMMY

What happened to King Hatshepsut? She simply disappears from history. Some say an impatient Thutmose III murdered her, but there is no evidence to support that theory. It is more likely that Hatshepsut died a natural death and then Thutmose III took his place as king of Egypt. Up until this point we are in the dark—there are no tales told.

❝ Tomb inscription of an army scribe, Deir el-Bahari, about 1479 BCE

Five shiploads of Egyptian marines forced the Puntites into an uneven trade. In exchange for a few beads and blades, the Egyptians brought home gold, ivory, animal skins, resins to make incense, trees, and exotic animals.

BIGGER AND BETTER

Karnak began during the
Middle Kingdom as a
shrine and was added onto
for 2,000 years until the
religious complex's temples,
columns, and statues cov-
ered 250 acres. Hatshepsut
and Thutmose III both
built at Karnak, erecting
obelisks and temples to
hold their stories.

the "Via Maris" (the Way of the Sea), which was the most
important road running between Egypt in the south, and all
of the countries to the north. Thutmose III's first military
mission was to capture Megiddo.

Thutmose III joined his army at a fortress on Egypt's
border and marched at a frantic pace toward Megiddo. On
their way to the city they came to a place where the road

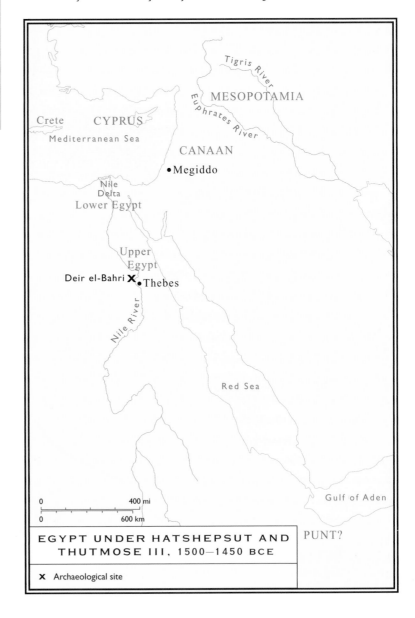

EGYPT UNDER HATSHEPSUT AND THUTMOSE III, 1500–1450 BCE

X Archaeological site

divided in three. Here a decision had to be made. One road snaked north and east, ending miles away from Megiddo. One road meandered north and west, curving miles off course and also ending miles away from Megiddo. The third route was a direct route. It headed straight north, ending near the gates of the city. But there was a problem. The third route pinched through a narrow pass that would force the army to march single file. This left them vulnerable. What if they were ambushed while they were strung out in a long line that couldn't be defended? The rebels would pick them off one by one. From inscriptions at Karnak we know Thutmose III's war council begged him, "do not make us go on the difficult road!" But of course the bold Thutmose III did. "Then his majesty commanded the entire army to march upon the road which threatened to be narrow. He went forth at the head of his army himself, showing the way by his own footsteps; horse behind horse, his majesty being at the head of his army." Thutmose III led his troops through the dangerous pass.

The rebel forces never expected the Egyptian army to choose the dangerous direct road. They had divided the bulk of their army between the other two roads, leaving the central pass virtually unprotected. When the Egyptians attacked, the enemy retreated to the city gates of Megiddo, "they fled headlong to Megiddo with faces of fear. They abandoned their horses and chariots of gold and silver. . . . " Slow runners found the gates already slammed shut and had to be pulled over the walls by their friends inside, using ropes made from clothes tied together. Thutmose III's daring dash worked.

Because the Egyptians stopped to collect the loot abandoned by the fleeing soldiers, victory was not theirs that day. They were forced to wait outside the city walls for what, according to the records, was a seven-month siege. But the day's events sent a message to the ancient world. The throne of Egypt was in capable hands with the warrior king Thutmose III in control. Egypt would flourish under him. Its territory would be greatly expanded. *Ma'at* would be maintained. For Egypt it would be a golden age.

FIRST BATTLE

The battle of Megiddo, fought in 1479 BCE, is the first battle in history whose details were written down so that we can follow the action from beginning to end.

❝ Inscription at Karnak temple, Luxor, about 1479 BCE

❝ Inscription at Karnak temple, Luxor, about 1479 BCE

IN STYLE ALONG THE NILE
DAILY LIFE

Egyptians had no word for "art." Everything decorative had purpose or meaning. On this tunic the painted cow walking east—away from the tombs west of the Nile—represents the goddess Hathor being reborn.

Ancient Egyptians didn't worry about ending up on the worst-dressed list. No one appeared in carvings on the temple walls with a blurry blob over his face to mask the identity of a "fashion don't." But that's not because Egyptians weren't into grooming. The Greek historian Herodotus wrote that they were obsessed with it. The Egyptians weren't concerned about what to wear because, unlike today, where styles change every season, Egyptian fashion remained the same for thousands of years.

So what would an Egyptian fashion magazine look like (other than the fact it would be written on papyrus, need only one issue every 1,000 years or so, and could only be read by a few people since only about 1 percent of Egyptians could read)?

The cover girl's head would be shown in profile—that was how Egyptian artists drew people. She would be wearing a simple linen tube called a *kalasiris* that fell loosely to just above her ankles. If a man posed for the cover, he'd be dressed in a linen skirt, or *schenti*, that wrapped around his hips. That's what people wore, rich or poor. *How* the outfit was made could be quite different, though. If you happened to be royalty, your *kalasiris* or *schenti* would be woven from the finest plants, called flax, into a sheer, flowing, baby-soft linen. Weavers might then embroider the linen with thread of spun gold. If you happened to be an unskilled laborer, your clothes would be a bit scratchy because the fabric was woven from coarse vegetable fibers.

An ancient fashion magazine would certainly have ads for jewelry. Ancient Egyptians loved their jewelry, especially rings. They wore two or three on every finger. Even the poorest class wove grass and wildflowers for necklaces, bracelets, and rings. Jewelry wasn't just for women. Men were just as fashion conscious. Many male mummies have pierced ears. The king awarded his soldiers and faithful followers with large hoop earrings and gold jewelry known as "Gold of the Brave."

One good reason to accessorize was that jewelry had supernatural powers. Egyptians believed that gold was the flesh of the sun god, Re. And silver, which was rare in Egypt and even more precious than gold, was thought to come from the bones of the moon god. Heavy golden collars were engraved with spells. The enchanted collars brought joy, health, and strength to the wearer. Jewelry could protect the wearer from dangers, too. Children wore fish-shaped jewelry in their hair to prevent drowning. The cobra on the king's crown symbolically spit venom at his enemies. Now that's a fashion accessory!

What would a fashion magazine be without those scratch-and-sniff perfume ads? Priests in ancient Egypt were the first chemists, concocting secret fragrance formulas and creamy eyeliners to sell to those who could afford them. The priests' perfumes were popular with everybody who was anybody and became a valuable export for Egypt. There was no money yet, but the priests traded for whatever they needed—linen, oils, even land. Scented body oils were so valued that they were often used as wages for workers. Popular fragrances were cinnamon, lily, and vanilla, but the priests didn't just use oils from plants, they used oils from hippos, crocodiles—even cats. To be the hit of any banquet, you needed a scented wax cone to tie on top of your head. As the evening wore on the wax melted down the sides of your face and wig, perfuming the air.

A wax cone on your head wasn't the only "must have" party accessory. Men and women showed up at banquets with their cosmetic chests, keeping them nearby to touch up their makeup. The chests themselves were works of art with inlaid jewels and painted scenes. Inside, the Egyptians kept a mirror called a "see-face" made from polished copper—or if you were really rich, silver. Wealthy women carried their see-face in a mirror bag over their shoulders. You might pack your cosmetic chest with bronze tweezers to

King Tut had several pairs of earrings placed in his tomb to wear in the afterlife. It was not unusual for men in ancient Egypt to have pierced ears and wear earrings.

FINE JEWELRY

Egyptian jewelers used semiprecious stones. Diamonds, rubies, and emeralds had not yet been discovered.

A wig as elaborate as this one would only be worn by the wealthiest Egyptians. In this case it was fit for a queen—literally.

66 New Kingdom love poem, about 1570–1070 BCE

Hand mirrors were not only functional, they had meaning, too. The round mirror symbolized the sun. The handle, in the shape of a papyrus stalk sprouting the face of the fertility goddess Bat-Hathor, represents rebirth.

pluck your eyebrows and hairpins made of ivory. You would definitely include a flat stone palette to crush black and green rocks into powder for eyeliner. Everyone wore heavy eyeliner. Men and women were already wearing eye make-up by the time the pyramids were built. As a popular New Kingdom love poem says, "I wish to paint my eyes, so if I see you my eyes will sparkle." So much for the natural look. Chemists from modern cosmetic companies have found that ancient Egyptians used the same proportion of fat as they do today to give their eye makeup that luxurious creamy texture.

What would our ancient fashion magazine say about hair? It would probably advise us to get rid of it. Men and women either shaved their heads or kept their hair cropped very short. In a climate where fleas and head lice thrived, this was practical hair-care practice. Archaeologists found a wig workshop at Deir el-Bahri along with several wigs. Like clothing, the quality of the wig depended on your station in life. The best wigs were shoulder length, made from as many as 120,000 human hairs woven into a mesh cap and fixed in place with beeswax. Some were ironed straight, others curled into ringlets, and for the really wealthy, braided with beads and jewels. If you weren't able to afford a good wig, yours might be made from palm fronds.

Although Egyptians kept their hair short, they were concerned about what hair they did have. The Ebers Papyrus has recipes for hair care. To strengthen hair, a mixture of crushed donkey teeth and honey is recommended. To prevent graying, it advises applying the blood of a black animal accompanied by a spell that transfers the black from the animal to the hair. For hair loss it says: "Recipe to make the hair of a bald person grow: fat of lion, fat of hippopotamus, fat of crocodile, fat of cat, fat of serpent, and fat of ibex are mixed together and the head of the bald person is anointed therewith." A more straightforward cure for baldness was the application of chopped lettuce to the bald spot.

You would think a place where people went out and about with chopped lettuce on their heads would have absolutely no "fashion don'ts," but there were definite no-nos.

Fashion don't: Wool or leather in temples or in front of the king. Remember, the gods were often part animal. It was not in good taste to be wearing animal parts to worship. Wool from sheep and goats was considered unclean, so it was never worn next to the skin. Although cloaks were made of wool, they were always worn over linen.

Fashion don't: Wearing shoes outdoors. Always carry your shoes on a journey and put them on when you arrive at your destination.

Fashion don't: Facial hair. Beards were considered unclean (remember the fleas and lice) and the mark of a barbarian. The one exception to this fashion don't was the braided fake beard worn by the pharaoh—but then who is going to criticize the pharaoh's fashion sense?

It is no wonder Herodotus thought that Egyptians were obsessed with their appearance. Tomb walls show their dedication to grooming. A nobleman who lived nearly 4,500 years ago is shown getting a pedicure. At Deir el-Bahri there is scene after scene of royal cosmetic rituals. The number

Ebers Papyrus, about 1550 BCE

FOOTWEAR

Egyptians went barefoot even at the fanciest parties. But if they wore shoes, they would most likely be sandals. Sandals found in one king's tomb had pictures of his enemies on the soles. When the king walked, he trampled them.

and quality of cosmetic containers and palettes found in tombs is more evidence of the importance Egyptians placed on good grooming. One fabulous makeup jar was carved so delicately that the alabaster is nearly transparent. This 6th dynasty (about 2345–2180 BCE) cosmetic container is in the shape of a female monkey cradling her baby in such a way that it looks as if it is in her womb.

The Ebers Papyrus also has practical advice on how to manage body odor. "To expel stinking of the body of man or woman: ostrich-egg, shell of tortoise and gallnut from tamaris are roasted and the body is rubbed with the mixture." For those looking for a simpler deodorant, the trend was to roll incense into a ball and mash it into your armpits. From body oils to body paint, Egyptians had a bounty of beauty hints—honey for anti-wrinkle cream, mint for fresh breath, beeswax for hair gel.

If ancient Egyptians had an advice columnist, it would likely be "Dear Bes." Bes was the mischievous god of the family. Picture a god that is part dwarf, part lion—stocky, with a big head, bugged-out eyes, sticking his tongue out at you. That's Bes. Bes rarely walked. He skipped, hopped, or danced—and none too gracefully—while playing his tambourine. Everyone loved Bes.

Dear Bes,
"I am a free woman of Egypt. I have raised eight children, and have provided them with everything suitable to their station in life. But now I have grown old and behold, my children don't look after me anymore." What should I do?

Sincerely,
Geezer from Giza

Dear Geezer,
This is Egypt. Women have more legal rights than anywhere else in the world. You own your own property and can do what you want with it. Cut the ungrateful kids out of your will.

Bes

66 Ebers Papyrus, about 1550 BCE

66 Last will and testament of Lady Naunakhte, about 1151–1145 BCE

Dear Bes,
My neighbor keeps stealing the grain we keep up on the roof. Is there anything we can do to stop her?

Sincerely,
Hungry in Hermopolis

Dear Hungry,
Theft is a big problem in village life. You probably can't stop her from stealing, but you could have a little fun and make her hair fall out. Try this recipe from the Ebers Medical Papyrus: "To cause the hair to fall out: burnt leaf of lotus is put in oil and applied to the head of a hated woman."

Bes

Bes stomps his feet and shakes his tambourine to frighten off evil spirits, and if that doesn't work, he sticks out his tongue. Bes was the god of the welfare of the family, particularly protective of newborns.

66 Ebers Papyrus, about 1550 BCE

Our magazine wouldn't have a wedding section. There is no evidence that ancient Egyptians had a marriage ceremony—no religious ceremony, no legal ceremony, no vows or rings, no wedding gown. A woman moved into her husband's house and took over from the mother the title of "woman of the house." Bes would get a lot of letters asking advice about how to get along with the mother-in-law! A marriage contract listed what the woman brought with her so that if there was a divorce the property could be split up properly. If divorced, women were entitled to what they brought into the marriage plus a share of the joint property.

Our magazine would have book reviews. Thumbs up for *The Tale of the Shipwrecked Sailor*, the action-packed adventure of a sailor marooned on a deserted island. Or is it deserted? When a giant human-headed serpent appears

The Tale of a Shipwrecked Sailor, 12th dynasty manuscript, about 2000 BCE

The Story of the Eloquent Peasant, Middle Kingdom manuscript, about 2040–1782 BCE

New Kingdom love song lyrics, about 1570–1070 BCE

Herodotus, *Histories*, about 450 BCE

the sailor realizes he's not alone. "Then I heard a noise of thunder; I thought it was a wave of sea, for the trees were splintering, the earth shaking. I uncovered my face and found it was a serpent coming." Twist ending leaves the reader hanging.

Thumbs down for *The Story of the Eloquent Peasant*. Whining, complaining peasant makes a meteoric climb from poor peasant to the pharaoh's right-hand man in this unbelievable tale of rags to riches. After the ninth time, the peasant complains to the pharaoh about all the injustices he has suffered, the reader identifies much too closely with the line "while for him who longs to see it come, death comes slowly." The reader is wishing for a crocodile to come along and swallow the peasant just to shut him up. The pharaoh must be terribly bored to enjoy the peasant's story so much that he rewards him with wealth and status. At least the peasant stopped complaining.

The Egyptians loved music, so there surely would be music reviews. "When I see you my eyes shine and I press close to look at you, most beloved of men who rules my heart. Oh, the happiness of this hour, may it go on for ever! . . . Never leave me!" If those love-song lyrics don't get your toe tapping, how about these lyrics from a New Kingdom love song? "Oh, night, be mine forever, now that my lover has come."

No magazine would be complete without a horoscope. Herodotus writes, "The Egyptians have ascertained the god to whom each month and day is sacred and they can therefore tell, according to the date of the child's birth, what fate is in store for him, how he will end his days, and what sort of person he will become." The calendar had lucky days and unlucky days. The unlucky days were "days of the demons." But if you were born on the 10th day of the 4th month of the Inundation, your destiny was to live to a ripe old age— now that's a lucky day.

That's it for this issue. Look for the next edition next millennium, when fall fashions take on a Greek look.

NAME THAT TOMB
AMENHOTEP III AND THE GOVERNMENT OF EGYPT

❝ COMMEMORATIVE SCARABS, TOMB INSCRIPTIONS FROM VIZIER OF THE FIRST INTERMEDIATE PERIOD, AMENEMHET'S TOMB, AND DIODORUS SICULUS

A ncient Egyptians recognized the importance of the right name. It announced to the world who you were, where you came from, and what was expected of you. Almost all of the kings from the 18th dynasty had the birth names Amenhotep or Thutmose. Their names showed the world that they pleased the gods. Amenhotep links the king with the sun god Amun— it means, "Amen (or Amun, or Amon depending on how you choose to spell it) is satisfied." Thutmose links the king with the god of wisdom Thoth— it means "Thoth is born." By the Middle Kingdom, kings were adding four official names to their birth name, but they could add many, many more. If you could give yourself a few more names, what might you choose? Amenhotep III liked to call himself "The Dazzling Sun Disk." Historians have nicknamed him "Amenhotep the Magnificent." Not bad for a child-king who began his reign when he was only 10 or 12 years old.

If you were forced to pick one word to sum up the essence of a king's rule, you might pick "trade" for Hatshepsut's time in power, "conquest" for Thutmose III's reign, and for Amenhotep III the word might be "diplomacy." From the start Amenhotep III made sure the world knew about him. In a time without newspapers or television, getting the word out about your accomplishments wasn't easy. Amenhotep III used beetles. Not live beetles— fake beetles. These pocket-size, turquoise-glazed stones, carved in the shape of beetles called scarabs, bore testimony

Even 3,350 years ago, people were obsessed with having a youthful appearance. Artists usually tried to show the king as "just right"—not too young and not too old—but the older Amenhotep III grew, the younger they seemed to portray him.

Pharaohs frequently issued scarabs, which looked like large beetles, to commemorate important events in their reigns. These scarabs were too large to be worn; they were probably displayed on a table, perhaps as a papyrus weight.

" Commemorative scarab, about 1385 BCE

" Commemorative scarab, about 1385 BCE

REGNAL YEARS

Egyptians recorded dates differently than we do. Each time a new king took the throne the year was reset to one. Although their calendar had 365 days in a year as ours does, it had no leap year. Over centuries that discrepancy of one day adds up. This is why there is dispute over the dates of reigns in terms of our calendar. The further we go back in time, the less reliable our estimates are.

on their bellies. Details of Amenhotep III's big moments were inscribed on their undersides. Because dozens of these scarabs have been found in neighboring countries scholars call them imperial news bulletins.

The first commemorative scarab from Year 2, 1385 BCE (two years into his reign would make Amenhotep III at most 14) is known as the Marriage Scarab. The inscription begins with all five of Amenhotep III's names. It then names his wife, "The great royal-wife Tiy... she is the wife of the mighty king...." The second scarab, also commissioned in Year 2, announces Amenhotep's second love—big-game hunting, a favorite royal pastime. When the young king heard that wild bulls had been spotted, he traveled by night along the Nile for the hunt. The wild-bull-hunt scarab claims: "a marvelous thing took place." Although Amenhotep III probably looked regal in his chariot pulled by the most magnificent horses in the country, *marvelous* might be a bit much. The animals were penned, so the "hunt" didn't require much hunting. Still, shooting arrows and throwing javelins from a chariot racing full tilt takes skill. And Amenhotep III would want to spread the word that he was indeed a skilled hunter. Egyptians believed that if their king was successful as a hunter, he would be successful on the battlefield. Hunting meant much more than killing a beast, it meant winning against the forces of chaos. That's a tall order for such a young man. It's no wonder he sent beetles scurrying throughout the ancient world to tell of his triumphs.

The mere mention of a name can be significant. In Year 10, a scarab was distributed announcing the arrival of a foreign princess to join Amenhotep's harem. But even on this scarab commemorating another woman, Queen Tiy's name is the name most closely linked to the king. Putting their names together clearly announces to the world her position as first queen. The last scarab, put out in Year 11, confirms their close relationship. It describes how a devoted Amenhotep III orders a lake made for his queen, Tiy. The lake was more than a mile long and a quarter of a mile wide. Some scholars estimate it may have been dug in just 15 days. "His Majesty celebrated the feast of the opening of the lake" by sailing with his queen on the royal barge named his favorite name—the Dazzling Sun Disk.

Commemorative scarab, about 1386–1349 BCE

Amenhotep the Magnificent was a very lucky king. He came to the throne when Egypt's treasury bulged with surplus harvests, the spoils of war, and goods from trade missions. And although the king would take sole credit for the country's good fortune, the man responsible for keeping things running smoothly was the vizier. Next to the king, the vizier was the most powerful person in Egypt. He, too, had many names, or titles. He was known as "Second to the King" and "Heart of the Lord" and "Eyes and Ears of the Sovereign." It was his job to keep law and order. He was in charge of taxes, all the records, troop movement, and even keeping track of the level of the Nile. The governors of every district reported to the vizier and the vizier reported to the king.

The vizier was a man who wore many hats (or, in at least two cases, *she* was a woman who wore many hats). As "Overseer of Works," the vizier was in charge of all of the king's engineering projects. He saw to it that men and materials were on site to build monuments, tombs, and temples, to repair dikes, dig canals, and dredge waterways. As "Keeper of the Seal," the vizier was responsible for the records, for marriage contracts, wills, deeds to property, court transcripts, and keeping a head count of cattle and people. His duties were endless. One vizier didn't exaggerate when he wrote, "I spent many hours in the service of my lord."

Tomb inscription from vizier of the First Intermediate Period, probably Thebes, about 2181–2040 BCE

The vizier served the king, the gods, and the people. An 18th-dynasty scribe writes that the vizier

Text from the tomb of Amenemhet, scribe to User, Valley of the Nobles, about 1504–1450 BCE

> Did what the king loves: he raised ma'at to its lord.... reporting daily on all his effective actions....

> Did what the gods love: he enforced the laws and laid down rules, administered the temples, provided the offerings, allotted the food and offered the beloved ma'at....

Did what the nobility and people love: he protected both rich and poor, provided for the widow without a family and pleased the revered and the old.

All this work was too much for one person. Many officials reported to the vizier. And each of them had a title, usually with the name "overseer." There was the "Overseer of the Double House of Silver" (the treasurer), the "Overseer of the King's House" (the royal steward), and there was even the "Overseer of the Royal Toenail Clippings" (no explanation necessary). The officials who came in contact with the king personally could add yet another name to their title that meant, "Known to the King" (an addition the Toenail Clipping official most likely deserved).

Originally the job of vizier was given to the sons of the king, but by the New Kingdom any official could rise to the position. It was possible for an ambitious commoner to become vizier, and it was possible for a vizier to become king. In times of turmoil, when weak kings ruled, it was the vizier who held Egypt together. A particularly powerful or a

The stone at the very top of a pyramid is called a capstone. The capstone's base is carved out like the bowl of a spoon, and the stone it sits on fits perfectly inside, holding the capstone in place.

particularly talented vizier might serve more than one king-ship. This had the advantage of making the royal change-over a smooth one.

One of the vizier's primary jobs was to uphold justice. Ancient justice doesn't sound like justice at all to us. It sounds brutal. Because tomb images paint a picture of life the way Egyptians hoped it would be in the afterlife, popular impressions of ancient Egypt are rose colored. No one likes to commemorate their failures, especially on beetles and certainly not on their tomb walls. Not only that, Egyptians believed anything written came true. Believing that, one would surely be very careful what they wrote. Egyptian life was not the idyllic paradise so many would like to believe. It had a dark side.

In Amenhotep's time, the top 5 percent of the popula-tion controlled the wealth of Egypt. At the head of it all, of course, was the king. Ranked below him were the vizier and several hundred families who ran the country as priests and overseers. Just below these elite families was a growing upper-middle class of educated people. And below them was the bulk of the population—people who were tied to the land, illiterate and unskilled. As the middle class grew, it became more and more worried about protecting its wealth. Punishments for robbery became more severe.

The most extreme punishment was death and destruc-tion of the corpse so there would be no entry to the after-life. Execution was a cheap way of getting rid of criminals. Egyptians were not willing to pay to house and feed law-breakers. Prisons were used only for those waiting for trial or waiting for their punishment. They were never used as they are today *as* the punishment. If the punishment was execution, the method was most often impalement on a wooden stake or, less often, burning. The most severe pun-ishments were applied to crimes against the state. It wasn't wise to mess with the king's property—and, technically speaking, everything in Egypt belonged to the king. The king would not tolerate such a challenge to his authority. The offender was punished not only as an example to oth-ers, but also to reaffirm the king's supreme power.

HAREMS

During the New Kingdom, so many women and children were associated with the king that they needed their own place to live. Today archaeologists are studying one harem palace known as Mer-Wer. It was home to an entire community of women, chil-dren, scribes, administra-tors, and servants. Mer-Wer was financially independ-ent, owning the farms sur-rounding it.

As the right-hand man to the pharaoh, a vizier's work is never done. The wall painting in this vizier's tomb shows the woodcarvers and carpenters who were under his watch hard at work.

❝ Diodorus Siculus, *Histories,* about 90–21 BCE

PAY YOUR TAXES— OR ELSE!

The first person in Egypt identified by name (Mery) for tax evasion was sentenced to 100 blows for his crime.

Government investigators had the right to arrest and question suspects. If they doubted the testimony of a witness, they had the right to torture him, and the investigators didn't hesitate to do it. Peasants accepted flogging as a part of life. Teachers beat students, overseers beat servants, police beat suspects. Even tax collectors were armed with sticks for beating tax delinquents.

For every crime the courts assigned a specific punishment. For example, the penalty for stealing cattle was amputation of the nose and ears, with hard labor for the thief and his wife and children. Floggings, assignment to labor gangs, and amputation of noses and ears were the most common criminal sentences. Those who were sentenced to work in the quarries and mines suffered a fate far worse; only half of them survived the trek through the desert. The Greek historian Didorus Siculus recorded Egyptian court judgments: "The penalty for perjury was death; the reasoning being that the perjurer was guilty of the two greatest sins, being impious towards the gods and breaking the most important pledge known to man."

These are not the stories that cover the walls of the tombs of kings and nobles. They are written in the court documents and stored in the prison archives. They are not inscribed on the bellies of beetles. Who we are, where we are going, and what we've done are not always what we want to announce to the world. Our dark side is not something we want named. But in real life even sweet-smelling roses have thorns. So it was with real life in ancient Egypt.

CHAPTER 14

DIPLOMACY MAKES GOOD FERTILIZER

FOREIGN RELATIONS DURING THE NEW KINGDOM

What we know about how Egypt got along with its neighbors came to us quite by accident. In 1887 a peasant woman was poking through the ruins of an ancient city we now call Amarna. She was collecting the crumbled remains of mud bricks, which make excellent fertilizer. Digging through the rubble she came across a stash of tablets. The hunks of sun-dried clay looked more like dog biscuits a chicken had pecked than treasure, but the woman collected the unbroken ones on the off chance she could get a few small coins for them. She gathered as many as she could carry and sold them to her neighbor. The neighbor turned around and sold them for a slight profit to a local dealer in antiquities. No one knew what they were, or if they had any value.

Rumors of this odd discovery spread. Museum curators in the major European cities were curious. Were these tablets ancient? Were they records of some sort? Or was this just another money-making hoax? The curators sent scouts to Egypt to find out. The scouts had orders to buy as many tablets as they could if they turned out to be genuine. The British Museum sent Budge.

E. A. Wallis Budge knew the tablets were in the hands of native dealers, but just who those dealers were would not be easy to find out. Government officials in the Egyptian antiquities department had announced plans to seize the tablets and throw anyone connected to them in jail. The dealers weren't about to give up the tablets for nothing, and they didn't intend to go to prison either. Threats only made them stubborn. What tablets? They didn't know anything about tablets found at Amarna. The Egyptian official in charge, Monsieur Grebaut, just threatened louder. Anyone

From 1894 to 1924, E. A. Wallis Budge was the curator of Egyptian Antiquities at the British Museum. Budge is best known for translating the Book of the Dead, the Egyptian guidebook for entrance into the afterlife. Budge was knighted in 1920.

Greek travelers named these 60-foot-tall statues of Amenhotep III the Colossi of Memnon. Memnon was the son of the Greek goddess of the dawn. After an earthquake cracked the right statue, it began to moan at sunrise. Legend has it that the sound was Memnon saying good morning to his mother.

refusing to co-operate would be tortured. The dealers didn't trust anyone. Budge hoped he could draw them out. Today reputable museums do not buy looted antiquities, but back in Budge's day that was how things were frequently done.

When Monsieur Grebaut's spies reported to him that Budge was in Egypt, he knew it must be about the tablets. He had Budge shadowed. The police reported Budge's every move to Monsieur Grebaut. Budge couldn't step outside his hotel room without being followed. Every antiquities dealer who met with Budge was investigated. When Budge traveled by train, the police climbed aboard, too. Monsieur Grebaut hoped Budge would lead him to the tablets.

In Luxor, while negotiating with a local dealer over a papyrus, word reached Budge that warrants for his arrest and the arrest of any dealer seen speaking to him were on their way. When Budge asked how long before the warrants arrived, the messenger explained that Monsieur Grebaut was bringing the warrants himself, traveling by steamer down the Nile. After coffee and more polite questions, the messenger told the whole story. It seems Monsieur Grebaut had not learned his lesson about threats. Single-minded in his quest to get Budge and the tablets, he had ordered the steamer captain to push on to Luxor and pass by the town where the captain's daughter was getting married. Just as they passed the captain's hometown the steamer "accidentally" ran aground on a sandbar. No matter how hard they tried, for some reason no one could free the steamer. It looked as if it wasn't going anywhere, at least until the wedding was over.

Frustrated, Monsieur Grebaut scoured the village for a donkey to hire so that he could ride the 12 miles to Luxor and arrest everyone who was mixed up in the whole tablet mess. But, oddly, there was not one donkey to rent anywhere in the village.

The messenger told Budge (probably with a sly smile) that the villagers had driven all the donkeys into the fields so none would be available for the unpleasant Monsieur Grebaut.

Budge sipped his coffee without any hurry, knowing Grebaut would be held up at the least until the next day. And that afternoon, a dealer arrived, bringing six clay tablets with him. Were they *kadim* ("old")? he asked. Or *jaded* ("new")? Were the tablets genuine? Or were they fake? Budge writes in *By Nile and Tigris,* "When I examined the tablets I found that the matter was not as simple as it looked. In shape and form, and colour and material, the tablets were unlike any I had ever seen in London or Paris, and the writing on all of them was of a most unusual character and puzzled me for hours."

It was while he was puzzling over the wedge-shaped markings that he was able to make out the words, "to Nimmuriya, king of the land of Egypt." Budge writes, "The opening words of nearly all the tablets proved them to be letters or dispatches, and I felt certain that the tablets were both genuine and of very great historical importance." Budge stuck to his "letter" theory despite arguments from scholars who thought the tablets were fake and arguments from scholars who had misinterpreted the markings.

We now know that the tablets are indeed letters—letters addressed to the king of Egypt more than 3,300 years ago, and copies of the replies he sent back. Nimmuriya is none other than Amenhotep III. And those chicken scratches are

THE "A" LIST

In the ruins of Amenhotep's mortuary temple are the bases to what were once larger-than-life statues of the king. Now all that is left are his feet. Scholars believe counties and regions inscribed on the statues' bases are areas Amenhotep III was in contact with in some way. One of the bases lists locations in the Aegean, perhaps including the city of Troy. It is known as the Aegean List. Scholars can only guess the list's purpose, but it is another piece of evidence supporting Amenhotep III's value of diplomacy.

❝ Amarna Letters, about 1386–1334 BCE

This letter to Amenhotep III opens
with greetings from the king of
Mittani: "May everything be well for
you. . . . May everything be well for
your wives, your sons, your noblemen,
your chariots, your horses, your soldiers, your country and everything
belonging to you." The date is written
in black on the bottom of the letter—
much like our postmarks.

" Amarna Letters, about
1386–1334 BCE

" Amarna Letters, about
1386–1334 BCE

inscriptions written in the diplomatic language
of the time, the language of ancient Babylon.
Scholars today call the tablets the Amarna
Letters—a priceless collection of letters
between Egypt and its neighbors in the Near
East. The mud bricks the peasant woman
used for fertilizer once formed walls to an
ancient Egyptian foreign office at Amarna—
the House of the Correspondence of Pharaoh.
And the stash of tablets was a file full of
records stored there. Fewer than 400 survived
out of who knows how many. The letters
cover a timespan of nearly 30 years, from late
in Amenhotep III's reign into his son's reign.
The letters reveal greed and grievances. They
detail petty fights and political alliances—30
years of diplomatic correspondence between heads of state.

Scholars have divided the letters into two groups
according to the opening words that led Budge to believe
the tablets were letters. Some of the letters were between
the king of Egypt and independent foreign rulers who considered themselves the king's equal. They opened their letters by addressing the king as "brother."

The second group of tablets begins quite differently.
These senders wouldn't have dared to assume that they were
brothers of the king, but merely "your servant, the dust of
your two feet." The groveling continued for many lines.
These chiefs of foreign lands under the king's dominion, or
vassals, were so fearful of offending they don't even address
the king by name, but instead called him "my king, my sun."

Throughout history, alliances have been made through
marriage. Amenhotep III married several foreign princesses
in the name of diplomacy. But the Amarna Letters show that
Amenhotep III didn't consider these diplomatic unions a
give-and-take situation. When the king of Babylon asked for
an Egyptian princess, Amenhotep III flat out refused, even
though he had taken the king of Babylon's sister as a bride.
The angry king of Babylon wrote, "When I wrote to you about
marrying your daughter you wrote to me saying 'From time

immemorial no daughter of the king of Egypt has been given in marriage to anyone.' Why do you say this? You are the king and you may do as you please. If you were to give a daughter, who would say anything about it?" But Amenhotep III wasn't budging. Egypt did not give away princesses.

The marriages allied rulers, not countries. If either husband or father-in-law should die, negotiations started all over again. This letter from the King of Hatti to Amenhotep III's son, after Amenhotep III died, shows that things didn't always continue as they had in the past: "your father never neglected...the wishes I expressed, but granted me everything. Why have you...refused to send me...gifts of friendship, I wish good friendship to exist between you and me."

6 6 Amarna Letters, about 1386–1334 BCE

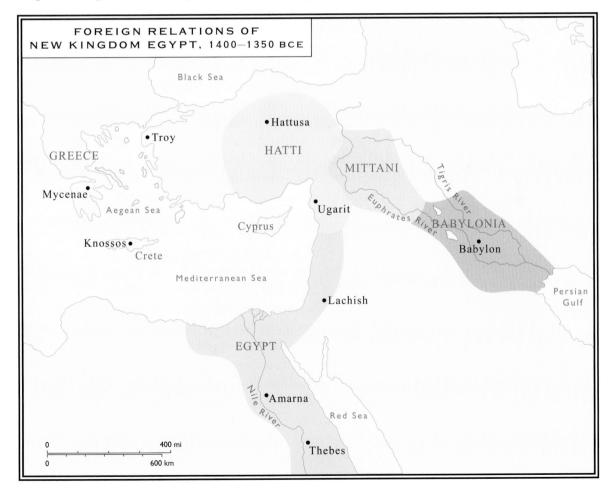

FOREIGN RELATIONS OF
NEW KINGDOM EGYPT, 1400–1350 BCE

Black Sea

• Hattusa

• Troy

HATTI

GREECE

MITTANI

Tigris River

Mycenae •

Aegean Sea

• Ugarit

Euphrates River

BABYLONIA

Cyprus

Knossos •
Crete

Mediterranean Sea

• Babylon

Persian
Gulf

• Lachish

EGYPT

Nile River

• Amarna

Red Sea

0   400 mi
0   600 km

• Thebes

Some of the letters were sent to people close to the king and pleaded for help. This letter from the king of Mittani to Queen Tiy shows how influential she must have been, not only during her husband's reign, but also during her son's:

Amarna Letters, about 1386–1334 BCE

You are the one who knows that I have always felt friendship for... your husband... but you have not sent me yet the gift of homage... your husband, has ordered be sent to me. I have asked... your husband for massive gold statues.... But your son has gold-plated statues of wood. As gold is like dust in the country of your son, why... [hasn't] your son... given them to me?

These are not the only letters of complaint. A constant theme throughout seems to be, "send more gold!" Or send more soldiers, more archers, more silver—diplomacy seems more like a greedy child's demands than true acts of alliance. The demands grew, and Amenhotep's son ignored them. Unlike Amenhotep III, his son's primary concern was not about foreign policy. Control outside of Egypt slipped, as the vassals were neglected and unable to support themselves. Undersupplied and discouraged, they pleaded for assistance, "your city weeps, and her tears are running, and there is no help for us. For 20 years we have been sending to our lord, the king, the king of Egypt, but there has not come to us a word from our lord, not one."

A tablet from Lachish, about 1386–1334 BCE

And what happened to Budge and Monsieur Grebaut? Did Budge end up in prison? Budge boarded a train for home with far fewer tablets than he would have liked. The lion's share had already been sold to the Berlin Museum. The dealer delivering a rather large tablet to his German contact in Cairo hid the 20-inch clay tablet in his clothes and covered himself with a large cloak. When the dealer climbed into the railroad car the tablet slipped from under his cloak and smashed into pieces on the ground. Informants passed the news to Monsieur Grebaut, who set out after that dealer and ordered everyone in sight to be thrown in jail. He telegraphed ahead the order to make the arrests. Surely he would be there soon... that is, if nothing stopped him.

CHAPTER 15

SUN WORSHIPPING
THE AMARNA PERIOD

Imagine your father owned the richest and most powerful country in the world. Not just ran it, *owned* it. It wasn't only the land that belonged to him, but also all the gold and grain in the treasury. He owned every brick in every building and every cow on every farm. The people and all that they owned were his as well. All of it one day would be passed down—but not to you, to your older brother. Since birth, he had been in training for the job while you watched from the sidelines. Tutors and generals and government overseers prepared your older brother for the day when he would take the reins. Your father, the king, and your mother, the queen, focused their attentions on your older brother, fussing over his every move, while you went unnoticed. That was life for Amenhotep IV, the second son of Amenhotep III.

Getting the lion's share of attention wasn't all good. You both learned to read and write, but when your brother was struggling with the language of diplomats, you could swish

Taxi anyone? The chariot was the mode of transportation for the royal family and their entourage around the city of Amarna.

Proverb used by students,
date unknown

your damp brush in the ink cake and practice your pen-manship on sayings like, "Report a thing observed, not heard." You both learned to drive a chariot, but while your brother had to practice looking regal, you could flush grouse out of the papyrus patch. The vizier grilled him on how each department in the government worked while you grilled the grouse.

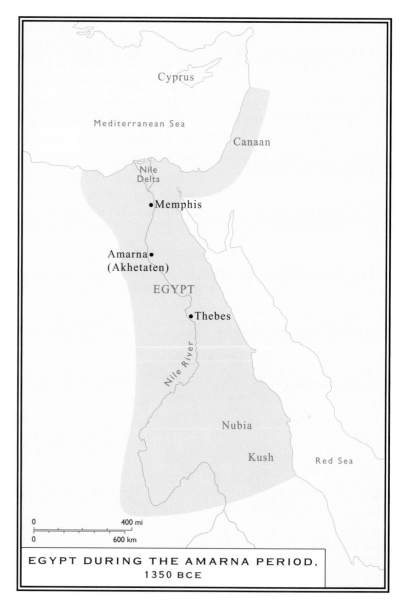

EGYPT DURING THE AMARNA PERIOD,
1350 BCE

When Amenhotep IV was a young boy, Egypt was . . . well, simply fabulous. The mid-1300s BCE was the golden age—literally. Gold flowed in from the Nubian mines so steadily that envious foreign leaders peevishly observed, "in my brother's country gold is as plentiful as dirt."

66 Amarna Letters, about 1386–1334 BCE

Egypt's empire stretched from Nubia to Syria. Tribute gifts flooded in from neighboring rulers who hoped to ally themselves with the powerful Egyptian king. Amenhotep IV must have watched a procession of riches being presented to his father. One ambassador after another laid gifts at his feet—exquisite jars from Crete, copper from Cyprus, jewels from Afghanistan, elephant tusks, giraffe skins, and ebony wood from Kush. Materialism was alive and well in Egypt. And everything had to be over the top. It wasn't enough to build a temple; the temple had to be COLOSSAL. A cloud of dust must have spread across Egypt from the dust raised by quarrymen and carvers, working the stone for all the buildings.

Traveling the Nile on the royal barge that was a floating palace, Amenhotep IV would have watched his father stop at town after town, performing rituals and paying tribute to the dozens of gods whose temples dotted the riverbank. Sailing against the current for the 400-mile trip from the northern capital of Memphis to the southern capital of Thebes would have taken three weeks without stops, but of course, there were always stops. Gratitude had to be expressed to the gods for Egypt's good fortune. That was the king's job. One day it would be Amenhotep IV's older brother's turn.

How different the two capitals must have seemed to young Amenhotep IV. In Memphis he wouldn't have been able to turn around without bumping into a scribe. Egyptians were compulsive record keepers. The archives bulged with their documents. A foreman couldn't hand out a loaf of bread to a workman without someone writing it down. Governors and overseers bustled through the streets of Memphis conducting Egypt's business, and the scribes recorded it all.

If Memphis were the brain of Egypt's operations, Thebes was its heart. Instead of government offices and business

CRUNCHY

Toothaches were common in all ancient cultures. But they weren't from eating too much sugar. Grains were ground with stones to make bread and porridge. Along with your meal there was always some grit and sand, not to mention the occasional rock-hard husk that had escaped grinding. A lifetime of tooth abuse wore away the protective enamel, making teeth vulnerable to decay.

❝ Homer, *Iliad*, about 750 BCE

ONE AND ONLY

Some scholars credit Amenhotep IV with being the first monotheist, or person who believes in one god. Although he is the first man we know of in history to speak of a single god, religion in Egypt 3,300 years ago was nothing like it is today. The gods gave no guidance or direction on how to live a good life. In fact, with all the lying, cheating, and murder (not to mention dismemberment) going on among the gods, they weren't even good role models.

Egyptian morality was not part of its religion. Scribes taught proper behavior, not priests. The role of religion in ancient Egypt is the same as the role of science today. We use astronomy and physics to explain why the sun rises each morning; the Egyptians used the gods. The gods explained the unexplainable.

centers, temples sprawled across the landscape. There were so many columns gracing so many entrances to so many temples that Homer called the city "Hundred-Gated Thebes."

When the royal barge docked at Thebes, priests would have greeted the king. What would Amenhotep IV have thought when he watched the power-hungry priests approach his father? Were they humble? Or had they grown too big for their kilts? The temples of Amun acquired more and more land with each passing year. Their farms were not meager vegetable plots feeding servants of the gods, but a thriving mini-kingdom lorded over by the priests. If the priesthood didn't eat away at his father's power, it certainly ate away at his father's treasury. With each conquest, Thebes received a share of the plunder. With every tribute or trade mission, Thebes took its cut. It was the gods' goodwill that had brought Egypt to this level of glory; payment was expected.

Although there were temples to many gods at Thebes, the main god of Thebes was Amun, "the hidden one." Amenhotep IV would have been left behind when his father followed the priests into the dark recesses of the inner temple. Only the holiest of holy could enter the inner sanctum where secret rituals were performed. Amenhotep IV was left out again.

Then, in a flash, everything changed. Amenhotep IV's older brother, groomed for the throne, died. All eyes turned to Amenhotep IV. And what did they see?

Some scholars believe that Amenhotep IV was a normal-looking young man. Their theory is that the distorted human forms artists began drawing at this time were the result of a new artistic style. The bodies, neither male nor female, but a bit of both, were meant to show the king as "everything." Other scholars have a different theory. They believe that Amenhotep IV was deformed by disease. They believe the long spidery fingers and toes, the head that looks like pulled taffy, and the stick arms, full breasts and sagging belly represent a true likeness. Amenhotep IV's mummy has never been found, but if one turns up with an unusual body shape, we'll know who it is.

Scholars aren't sure if Amenhotep IV ruled alongside his father for a short time or not. It would have been excellent on-the-job training for the inexperienced prince. It would also have made it crystal clear to anyone who might have designs on the throne that the job was filled. From Amenhotep III's mummy we know toward the end he was fat and in poor health. Two of his teeth on the right side were abscessed. He would have been in constant pain. With Amenhotep IV ruling beside him, Amenhotep III could escape the toothache with the latest painkiller from Cyprus—opium. If he had packed his teeth with opium, he would not have been able to make clear-headed decisions; a co-ruler would have been not only useful, but also necessary.

When Amenhotep III died, embalmers used a new method. They injected tree resin and salt under the skin to plump it up and give the body a more lifelike look. This innovation was the first in increasingly drastic changes that marked the reign of the rebel Amenhotep IV—a short blip in Egypt's history we know as the Amarna Period.

About the time that Amenhotep IV took the throne, he also took a wife—Nefertiti, which means "The Beautiful Woman Has Come." His parents' unusually close relationship could have been the model that led Amenhotep IV to break tradition again and share

Akhenaten holds the hand of his wife, Nefertiti. Some scholars believe that Nefertiti may have co-ruled with her husband. Others believe that although Nefertiti took an active role alongside her husband, there is no evidence that she shared his power.

his power with "the Foremost Wife of the King, whom he loves, the Mistress of the Two Lands, . . . Nefertiti, living and young, forever and ever." Amenhotep IV's devotion to Nefertiti was displayed on temple walls. Traditional paintings of the king as a muscled, fierce warrior were replaced with paintings of the king as a loving, doting family man— Amenhotep kissing his wife, Amenhotep with a daughter on his knee, Amenhotep surrounded by his family.

Soon Amenhotep IV found another obsession. He latched onto an obscure sun god that his father had fancied, Aten, which means "the disk." In the fifth year of Amenhotep IV's reign, he changed his name to Akhenaten which means "Spirit of the Sun Disk." The name change was not as shocking as what followed. Akhenaten announced that the gods Egyptians had been worshiping for thousands of years no longer existed. The Aten was the one and only. Akhenaten cut off funds to the temples. There would be no more tributes to these false gods, no more temples built in Thebes, no more revenues funneled into the priesthood. Those riches would now go directly to the Aten and (perhaps rather shrewdly) to his representative on Earth, the king himself—Akhenaten.

The way Queen Nefertiti's name and title are written on this scarab suggests that it is from the first five years of her rule as queen. After the fifth year, both she and her husband, Akhenaten, changed the spelling of their names to reflect their new worship of the god Aten.

The Aten needed his own city, a new capital built on new ground. Akhenaten sailed the Nile in search of the right spot to build the city. On the east bank of the Nile, halfway between Memphis and Thebes, a semicircle of cliffs rose above an arc of windswept desert. It was there, on an isolated strip of land, that Akhenaten built the city we know as Amarna.

Thousands of workers descended on Amarna, intent on raising a city. Brick makers poured mud from the riverbank into wooden molds then turned the bricks out to dry in the desert heat. Stone workers cut blocks from the quarries with bronze chisels and wooden mallets. In just four years the city was in full operation with commuters riding their donkeys from the suburbs in the north and south to the center of the city.

The largest structure in Amarna was the royal residence, of course. Built half on one side of the road, and half on the other, the east and west wings of the palace were connected by an overpass. The overpass was called the "Window of Appearances." From there Akhenaten, Nefertiti, and their children would greet the crowds gathered on the road below.

The new temple at Amarna was nothing like the old gloomy houses for the gods. The open courtyard allowed the Aten's rays to shine in. The rambling open-air place of worship stretched the length of two football fields, empty except for small stands to place food offerings, one for each day of the year.

Akhenaten's new capital was lined with office building after office building: the palace, the House of the Correspondence of Pharaoh, where the Amarna Letters were found; the police station, with a full staff of policemen who rode around in chariots; and a university, where priests of the new order were educated. Now that the old myths were no longer taught, Akhenaten had to write new ones. *The Great Hymn to the Aten* shows us Akhenaten's poetic side. He writes that even "Birds fly up to their nests, their wings extended in praise of your *ka* [spirit]." The hymn teaches that the Aten created not just Egypt, but the entire world and everything in it:

> You create the earth as you wish, when you were by
> yourself, . . . all beings on land, who fare upon their
> feet, and all beings in the air, who fly with their wings.
> The lands of Khor [Syro-Palestine] and Kush [Nubia]
> and the land of Egypt. . . . Tongues are separate in
> speech, and their characters as well; their skins are
> different, for you differentiate the foreigners.

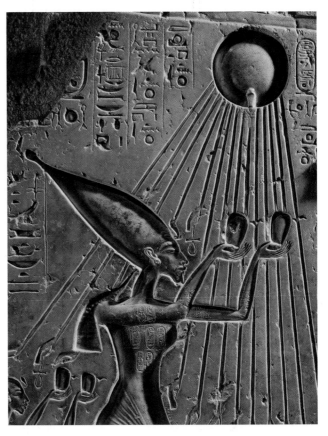

Akhenhaten's family worships Aten, the sun god. The Great Hymn to Aten *proclaims, "You rise in perfection on the horizon of the sky, living Aten, who determines life. Whenever you are risen upon the eastern horizon you fill every land with your perfection."*

‟ *The Great Hymn to the Aten,* about 1350–1334 BCE

Were Akhenaten's elongated features a deformity or an art form? Until his mummy is found, no one will know for sure.

The Great Hymn to the Aten, about 1350–1334 BCE

The hymn also makes it clear to the priests that they will *not* be the ones who represent the Aten on Earth, "There is no other who knows you except for your son [Akhenaten], for you have apprised him of your designs and your power."

Then Akhenaten took a fatal step. He denied Egyptians the afterlife. He doomed his new religion to failure. He had rankled the people by taking away the old gods and the old traditions, and now he took away their hopes for eternal life.

In his fervor for the Aten, Akhenaten forgot Egypt. The city of Amarna was like the royal firstborn son who took all the attention. The rest of Egypt became the second son, ignored and neglected. Egyptians outside Amarna were paying taxes to build a city they would never see, dedicated to a god they did not want.

Egypt's foreign subjects fell one by one to outside conquerors. The Amarna letters flooded in with pleas for help. They fell on deaf ears. One poor prince wrote at least 64 times, "Why will you neglect our land?"

Akhenaten had inherited an empire but left a country in decline. After his death the new capital was abandoned. The kings who followed Akhenaten demolished his temples and erased his name. Once Amarna had been stripped of stone it was forgotten and left to crumble. The sun had set on the Amarna Period.

NAME THAT TOWN

Akhenaten named the city Akhetaten, which means "Horizon of the Aten." We know it as Amarna, named for the tribe who lived there centuries later.

Amarna Letters, about 1386–1334 BCE

CHAPTER 16

ONLY TOMB WILL TELL
TUTANKHAMEN

Today when the body of a dead boy turns up, a team of specialists is sent to the scene. By examining the body, scientists can learn a great deal about that person's life, and often the cause of death. But in 1922, when archaeologist Howard Carter found Tutankhamen, no one thought a dead body had much to tell. In fact, people had so little regard for mummies that locals used them for firewood. Archaeologists sipped their afternoon tea by the fire with human bones—even skulls—at their feet. For scientists then, it was all about the tomb.

When Carter uncovered the first step to an ancient sunken stairway, he knew he had discovered the entrance to a tomb. But whose? On Sunday, November 5, 1922, Carter wrote in his diary, "The seal-impressions suggested that it belonged to somebody of high standing but at that time I had not found any indications as to whom."

A MUMMY A DAY KEEPS THE DOCTOR AWAY

For centuries ground-up mummy was a must-have in every medicine cabinet. People thought it was a miracle drug. They used it to treat everything from bruises to paralysis. King Frances I of France liked his mummy with rhubarb.

❝ Howard Carter, diary, November 5, 1922

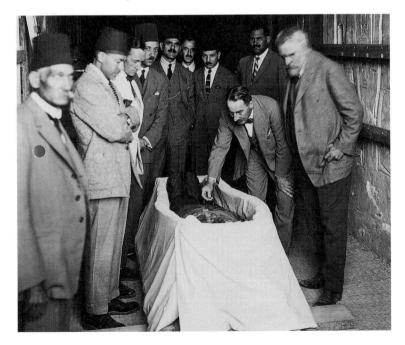

Howard Carter leans over King Tutankhamen's mummy. When people present at the opening of the tomb began to drop dead, including the person paying for the dig, rumors began that Tut had placed a mummy's curse on those who had disturbed him.

Howard Carter, diary,
November 24, 1922

When the workmen finished clearing the stairway on Friday, November 24, Carter wrote, "reached as far as the first doorway. There proved to be sixteen steps." After examining the first doorway, Carter found "various seal impressions bearing the cartouche of Tut-ankh-Amen." He had discovered King Tut's tomb.

Not much is known about Tutankhamen. He had taken the throne when he was only ten years old, and guided by his advisers, had set out to restore Egypt. But his father was probably the despised Akhenaten, the king who had robbed Egypt of its gods, and so Tutankhamen was guilty by association. The kings who followed him tried to erase the whole family from history.

Howard Carter, diary,
November 24, 1922

Carter's thrill at finding the tomb of this little known king quickly turned to dismay. The seals revealed that Carter wasn't the first to discover Tutankhamen's resting place. "In the upper part of this sealed doorway traces of two distinct reopenings and successive reclosings were apparent." This could mean only one thing—tomb robbers! With so much wealth heaped inside the royal tombs, it was impossible to keep thieves out. The priests of Amun had tried. They sealed the doors and filled the passageways with limestone chips, but still the robbers tunneled through.

After Carter passed through the first doorway, he found another descending passageway much like the first. Carter and his crew dug their way down the passage, every bucketful of rubble they removed bringing them closer to the second doorway. They must have wondered as they worked,

---

MIGHTY MONARCHS

1350–1334 BCE
Akhenaten

1336–1334 BCE
Smenkhkare

1334–1325 BCE
Tutankhamen

1325–1321 BCE
Ay

1321–1293 BCE
Horemheb

Tut's servants, or ushabtis, *wait to serve him in the afterlife. They hold the crook and flail, symbols of authority and power. Scholars believe the crook is a shepherd's staff and the flail is a shepherd's whip or flyswatter. Kings held them across their chests, symbolizing a shepherd leading his flock.*

would this be another disappointment? Would this be another once-glorious treasure-house, destroyed by thieves? What would they find?

Sunday, November 26

Howard Carter, diary, November 26, 1922

After clearing . . . the descending passage . . . we came upon a second sealed doorway, which was almost the exact replica of the first. It bore similar seal impressions and had similar traces of successive reopenings and reclosings in the plastering. The seal impressions were of Tut.ankh.Amen . . . Feverishly we cleared away the remaining last scraps of rubbish on the floor of the passage before the doorway, until we had only the clean sealed doorway before us. . . . we made a tiny breach in the top left hand corner to see what was beyond. . . . Perhaps another descending staircase . . . ? Or maybe a chamber? Candles were procured—the all important tell-tale for foul gases when opening an ancient subterranean excavation—I widened the breach and by means of the candle looked in. . . . It was sometime before one could see, the hot air escaping caused the candle to flicker, but as soon as one's eyes became accustomed to the glimmer of light the interior of the chamber gradually loomed before one, with its strange and wonderful medley of extraordinary and beautiful objects heaped upon one another.

The room Carter peered into was packed to the ceiling. A jumble of chests piled on top of chairs, piled on top of chariots. Statues, beds, game boards, and pottery littered the floor. Everything the king would need in the next life had been crammed into the small space. The tomb robbers must have been scared away before they could do much

RESTORATION

Tutankhamen's short reign was dedicated to restoration. He rebuilt the army, administration, temples, and trade agreements that his father had allowed to deteriorate. The army was enlarged, retrained, and outfitted with the latest weaponry, armor, and chariots. The administrative offices in Memphis were reopened and restaffed. Building began at the temple of Karnak. New trade agreements were negotiated. Restoration took revenue, so a new tax system was worked out. Peasants no longer were taxed on how much grain they grew, but on a rate officials determined they should grow. The rate was based on yearly nilometer readings.

damage. Carter writes, "we had found the monarch's burial place intact save certain metal-robbing."

But what was it they had found? If this was a tomb, where was the tomb resident? There were no mummies in sight. Carter writes, "A sealed doorway between the two sentinel statues proved there was more beyond, and with the numerous cartouches bearing the name of Tut.ankh.Amen on most of the objects before us, there was little doubt that there behind was the grave of that Pharaoh." The doorway to the burial chamber had been broken into as well. Carter writes that the hole was "large enough to allow a small man to pass through, but it had been carefully reclosed, plastered, and sealed. Evidently the tomb beyond had been entered— by thieves!" Would they find King Tut?

Before they could open the burial chamber, the antechamber had to be cleared. This was no small task. First, every object was photographed from all angles, recording their details and placement in the antechamber. The photographer's past experiences had taught him well. He told *The New York Times*, "I remember, when we were clearing a series of 18th Dynasty tombs, which had been infested with white ants, the preliminary photographs were literally the only record of most of the wooden objects found. The coffins appeared to be in perfect condition, but when touched they collapsed into dust."

Wood wasn't the only fragile material in King Tut's tomb. Linen crumbled in the excavators' hands. One garment embroidered with more than 50,000 beads needed special attention. If they touched the garment it would turn to dust and the beads would scatter. The pattern was recorded so that the beads could be put back in the same way on new linen. It took three weeks to empty a single chest of clothing. The antechamber took more than a year to empty.

Finally, Carter was able to break through to the burial chamber—and there he found a golden room. Four gilded shrines, each nested inside the next, boxed in King Tut's **sarcophagus**. When Carter took the shrines apart he noticed the hieroglyphs "front" and "rear" painted on the panels—assembly instructions. Whoever put the shrines

sarx + phagos =
"flesh" + "eating."
The Greeks believed a particular kind of stone ate flesh, so they make coffins out of the stone. A sarcophagus is essentially a flesh-eating box.

together must have ignored the instructions because the shrines were assembled backwards. The doors should have faced west so that King Tut could exit directly into the afterlife. They faced east instead. Poor Tut was turned around.

Carter pulled back the bolts on the innermost shrine's doors. Barely breathing, he swung open the doors. Inside, filling the entire shrine, was King Tut's stone sarcophagus. Winged goddesses carved into the yellow quartzite at each corner protectively embraced the sarcophagus and what lay within. The lid, however, was made from pink granite. Someone had painted it yellow to match the base. Had the original lid broken? This lid had cracked, too. The crack had been disguised with plaster and paint.

When Carter hoisted the lid to the sarcophagus, the likeness of Tutankhamen looked up at him from the seven-foot human-shaped coffin. The symbols of Upper and Lower Egypt—the cobra and the vulture—seemed to

Small gold mini-coffins held King Tutankhamen's internal organs. Because the face is not Tut's, some scholars believe that the container was intended for Tut's predecessor.

THE WORMS CRAWL IN, THE WORMS CRAWL OUT

Medical examination of mummies reveals that parasites were a problem for ancient Egyptians. The worms that plagued them weren't necessarily life threatening, but they were unpleasant. Guinea worms infected Egyptians through drinking water. Once inside the human body, a larvae matures into a three-foot-long worm, which painfully exits through the skin after a year. Strongyl worms enter the body through the feet and lay their eggs in the intestines, causing abdominal pain, and they migrate to the lungs and throat, causing a constant cough. Parasites didn't just infect the living, they fed on the dead as well. One mummy had more than 270 beetles in its skull.

sprout from Tut's forehead. And around the crown someone had lovingly placed a tiny flower wreath. The wreath was made of olive leaves, blue water-lily petals, and cornflowers.

When the workmen raised the coffin's cover, Carter began to worry. The coffin nested inside had been damaged by water. What if King Tut were badly damaged? Fearing the lid was too fragile to lift, Carter decided to remove the whole coffin. But when the workmen hoisted it, it was much heavier than it should have been. It wasn't until Carter opened the second coffin that he found out why. The third and innermost coffin was made of solid gold. It weighed 250 pounds.

When the last lid to the last coffin was finally raised, three years after the discovery of that first step sliced into the valley floor, Carter and King Tut were at last face to face.

66 Tutankhamen, Valley of the Kings, 1325 BCE

Howard Carter dusts off Tutankh-amen. Today the pharaoh is back in his original resting place, inside his three coffins. He is the only pharaoh left in the burial grounds the Valley of the Kings—at least the only one we know about!

Later, when Carter tried to put down on paper how he felt at that moment, he found he couldn't. There were no words to describe his intense emotions. He was overwhelmed by the realization that it had been more than 3,000 years since another human being had looked into the golden coffin.

The priests who performed Tut's funeral had poured sacred oils over the mummy and the coffin. The oils glued the two together. Carter tried to loosen the resin by warming it in the hot desert sun, but it was no use. Tut was stuck. They called in a professor of anatomy to perform the examination on Tut's remains. The professor sliced away the linen wrappings only to find that it wasn't just the wrappings stuck to the coffin. The body was stuck, too. First the professor tried to chisel away the body, and when that didn't work, he tried heated knives. Finally, he hacked the torso in half and removed the body by sections. How much would we have been able to learn using today's scientific methods had the body not been so brutally handled?

The arm and leg bones pulled from their joints allowed the professor to calculate King Tut's age. He was about 18 years old when he died. He was thin, and five feet six inches tall. Cause of death was never considered.

In a small side room, along with the jars that held King Tut's internal organs, Carter found two tiny coffins holding two tiny mummified fetuses. They were the mummies of the children Tut would never have—

This calcite chest holds four jars with stoppers crafted in Tut's likeness. The jars hold Tut's internal body parts. The brain was the only body part embalmers threw out, believing it was not essential. Everything else was saved for when it would return to the body in the afterlife.

his wife's miscarriages. The professor cracked open the skull of one. The embalmers had removed the brain and stuffed the hollow with linen. The professor found a wire that had been used to push the linen up into the skull, the only embalming tool ever found inside a body—and the professor threw it away.

If a mummy is discovered today, a team of scientists is sent to the scene. Botanists could have told Carter in what month King Tut died by studying the funeral wreath—cornflowers bloom in March in Egypt. Radiologists could have told Carter that King Tut did not die from tuberculosis as many had guessed, but may have been murdered by a blow to the back of the head. Or he may have fallen and hit the back of his head on the ground. King Tut's eye sockets were fractured in a way that is caused by the brain snapping forward when the head hits the ground in a backwards fall (or is clubbed from behind). Neurologists could have told Carter that the vertebrae in King Tut's neck were fused. When Tut turned his head, he had to turn his whole torso, too. Fibre-optic tubes with miniature cameras could have been inserted under the linen to take pictures and samples without ever having to unwrap Tut. Today scientists use DNA to reconstruct family trees. Computers re-create faces. And if we can learn that much more in the time since Carter discovered King Tut, imagine how much we will be able to learn in the future. The dead do tell tales. It's up to us to listen.

THE USUAL SUSPECTS

Who murdered King Tut? The most obvious suspects were those who had the most to gain from Tutankhamen's death, and they were his top three advisers. Was it Maya, the treasurer? Or was it Horemheb, the general? Or Ay, who in the end stole Tut's throne, wife, and tomb?

CHAPTER 17

SURVIVING CHILDHOOD
GROWING UP IN ANCIENT EGYPT

66 STRABO,
BERLIN PAPYRUS,
DELIVERY SAYINGS,
PROPHECY,
REGISTRATION
DECLARATION,
SCRIBAL ADVICE,
HEALING SPELL,
AND SONG OF THE
HARPIST

The prince standing behind the pharaoh has his hair fashioned in a sidelock. Girls and boys shaved their heads, leaving only one patch of hair on the side. This s-shaped side ponytail was part of the hieroglyphs meaning child, young, and youth.

66 Strabo, *Geography*, about 63 BCE–21 CE

No one in the ancient world loved their children more than the Egyptians. The Greeks, who sometimes left unwanted infants (most often girls) outdoors to die, were shocked to discover the Egyptians did not. The Greek geographer Strabo believed the fact "that they bring up all the children that are born" to be the Egyptians' most admirable quality. In Egypt, children (even girls) were considered a blessing. Pregnant women were fussed over, envied, and admired. And right behind them, the fathers stood all puffed up with their fatherhood. Egyptian men were loving fathers—and proud of it!

The medical document called the Berlin Papyrus, contains directions for the oldest-known pregnancy test. The test involves watering cereals with urine, and has a bonus feature of predicting the sex of the unborn child. "The woman must moisten it with urine every day. . . . If the barley grows it means a male child. If the wheat grows it will mean a female child. If neither grows, she will not give birth."

When it was time to deliver, women went to special birth houses. For the upper class, the birth house might be a luxurious room built next to the temple. For the less wealthy, the birth house might be a special room on the roof of the house where cool winds blew. Squatting with each foot on a large brick, or sitting in a special birthing chair with a hole in the seat, a woman gave birth assisted by female neighbors. The women in labor repeated prayers to Amun, "make the heart of the deliverer strong, and keep alive the one that is coming."

The dwarf-god Bes was a welcome sight to a woman in labor. Bes fought off evil spirits that might threaten her or her baby. During the Middle Kingdom, Bes's likeness might be carved onto the boomerang-shaped magic wand women often placed on their stomachs while giving birth. During the New Kingdom, Bes's picture might be painted on the birth house wall. Childbirth was dangerous to both mother and baby, so divine help from any of the gods associated with newborns was sought out, particularly from the chief god of newborns—the pregnant hippo-goddess, Taweret.

Scholars believe one out of every two or three newborns died, but they can only estimate because many newborns did not have their own burial. If a mother and baby both died in childbirth, they would be buried together. Babies who died soon after birth might be placed in clay pots and buried under the home, and those who never lived long enough to be named might be thrown into the Nile to the crocodiles. Mothers anxiously watched their babies for danger signs. With predictions such as, "If the child made a sound like the creaking of the pine trees, or turned his face downward, he would die," it's no wonder they were anxious.

Berlin Papyrus, about 1800 BCE

Delivery sayings, date unknown

Daddy Dearest

In Egypt 2,000 years ago, a Roman named Hilarion wrote this letter to his pregnant wife, which would have horrified Egyptian fathers:

I am still in Alexandria. . . . I ask and beg of you to take good care of our baby son, as soon as I receive payment I will send it up to you. If you deliver (before I get home), if it is a boy keep it, if it is a girl discard it. . . .

Prophecy, date unknown

Parents named their children quickly. A child without a name was doomed to the "second death"—complete erasure—no life after death. Mothers wasted no time announcing their newborn's name. Some names were long—Hekamaatreemperkhons. And some names were short—Ti. Some names described the child—Nefertiti, the Beautiful Woman Has Come. Some names connected the child with one of the gods—Tutankhamen, the Living Image of Amun. And some names were what the mother cried out when she gave birth—Nefret, pretty.

Ever the fastidious record keepers, Egyptians registered the child's name. All births, marriages, and deaths were recorded by the diligent scribes. Just as marriage required only a simple announcement to the proper authorities, so it was with a new child. To register a child the parents merely had to say something like what one princess said: "I gave birth to this baby that you see, who was named Merab and whose name was entered into the registers of the House of Life."

For the first three years a mother carried her baby around in a sling. One scribe tells children they should be appreciative. "Repay your mother for all her care. Give her as much bread as she needs, and carry her as she carried you, for you were a heavy burden to her." Breastfeeding for those first three years protected children from parasites in the drinking water. Digestive diseases were the most common illnesses for children. Mothers of sick children might recite this spell to ward off the evil spirit they thought to be the root of the problem: "Come on out, visitor from the darkness.... Have you come to do it harm? I forbid this! I have made ready for its protection a potion from the poisonous *afat* herb, from garlic which is bad for you, from honey which is sweet for the living but bitter for the dead."

In addition to using spells, parents would protect their children with amulets. Mothers hung a charm from a necklace—an ibis to heal, an eye to protect, or Bes to chase away evil spirits. Fathers paid scribes to write a protective spell on a tiny papyrus scroll that they would insert into a tube for the child to wear as a pendant. Each body part had its own god, so if a specific problem needed to be fixed, par-

" Princess Ahori, wife of Nenoferkaptah, registration declaration, date unknown

" New Kingdom scribal advice, "The Instructions of Ani," 1279–1212 BCE

" Healing spell, date unknown

ents could appeal to the appropriate god. Have an earache? Call in the Two Cobras. Broken arm? It's the Falcon you want. One poor young peasant must have had amulets hanging from everywhere. His name was Nakht.

Like most peasants, Nakht didn't go to school. He learned his father's trade by following him around from the time he was five years old. Children of wealthier families might have gone to scribal school, but not Nakht. He learned to be a weaver by being an apprentice. By the time he died, at the age of 15, he had probably been working on his own for years. We know a great deal about Nakht because he was *not* wealthy. Had his family been rich, they would have had him mummified. But mummification was expensive—too expensive for a poor weaver, even a weaver who worked in the king's temple. Yet after he died someone lovingly shaved Nakht's face, clipped his nails, wrapped him in linen and placed him in a humble wooden coffin. And there Nakht's body dried in the hot, dry climate.

Magical charms, or amulets, were supposed to protect their owners from injury. This wood carving of a mother and her baby lying in bed was worn by a mother during childbirth.

Today Nakht is not considered a poor humble peasant, but a priceless source of information about the health of children growing up during the New Kingdom. His brain is the oldest intact brain found to date. All his internal organs are in place. His heart is still attached to his ribcage and, even though his intestines are as delicate as tissue paper, they are there. So how healthy were young peasants weaving in Thebes? Not very.

Nakht would have been short of breath. He suffered from black lung disease and desert lung disease. Red granite dust irritated his lungs and in the end probably contributed to his death from pneumonia. A dark mass near his spleen indicates he had malaria. This and other parasites would have made him most uncomfortable. The worms traveled through his arteries and his intestines, and damaged his muscles, liver, and bladder, causing nausea, diarrhea, vomiting, fatigue, fever, headaches, chills, joint pain, and itchy skin. It's no wonder parents hung amulets around

❝ Healing spell, date unknown

their children's necks for protection and chanted spells such as, "The child should be safe from diseases, foreigners, bad-wishing Egyptians and dangerous waters."

Not all children suffered as much as Nakht. Paintings and inscriptions on tomb and temple walls show children having fun. They played hockey with sticks made from palm branches and pucks made from leather pouches stuffed with papyrus. Their dolls had real hair, miniature furniture, and clothes. Carefree childhood days were filled with tug-of-war, juggling, catch, board games, wrestling, fishing, and races. Even the poorest children had toys—tops, balls, boats, and animals with movable parts like a crocodile that opened and shut its toothed jaw or a leopard that wagged its tail. The climate being what it was, children often went naked (except for their amulets and jewelry) and shaved their heads (except for a lock on the right side).

Most children had pets to play with. All kinds of pets, from the familiar cats and dogs to the more unusual—monkeys, ducks, geese, falcons, and ferrets. Almost all modern cats are descendents from ancient Egyptian cats. Their word for "cat" was *myw*—meow! And, oh, how they loved their cats! Some parents named their children after their cats (especially the girls). Egyptians loved the mysterious and independent nature of cats. A favorite story has Egypt's enemies running in a frenzied retreat from hordes of cats. Cats were loved so much that for a time it was a crime to kill one. The penalty for killing a cat—even by accident—was death.

The ancient Egyptian word for dog also comes from the sound it makes—*iwiw*. But dogs were never revered like cats. It was an insult to be called "the pharaoh's dogs," and there are no images of a dog being petted.

Watch out—this toy cat bites. The cat's mouth opens and closes, and its pointy teeth are made of bronze. The Egyptians loved games and toys. One board game called senet pits players against the evil forces preventing entrance to the afterlife.

Students practiced writing on a piece of slate or clay that could be reused, much as a chalk board might be used today. They wrote with reed pens that were frayed at the end, which made them look like thin paintbrushes.

Still, leather collars marked with their names such as Brave One, Reliable, and Good Herdsman, prove that their owners valued them. (Except for that dog named "Useless"?)

For the lucky children, there was school (but it was rare for a girl to be that lucky). Education was a privilege for a select few. The majority of children never learned to read or write. Education began for children at about five years old. Those who did go to school walked, carrying a lunch of bread cakes and drinks. Or, if they were wealthy enough, tutors came to their home. During the Middle Kingdom, temples and palaces built Houses of Instruction where a chosen group of boys trained for their future jobs. In school, children sat cross-legged on the floor and recited passages over and over and over again. When they knew the sayings by heart they would write them over and over and over again. Papyrus was too expensive to waste on school children, so students practiced their penmanship with reed brushes and ink cakes (just like watercolors) on polished limestone or pieces of pottery. If tax collecting was in the student's future, he would learn arithmetic, too. Teachers expected their students to work hard and were quick to whip those who didn't. One scribe wrote, "Don't waste your day in idleness, or you will be flogged. A boy's ear is on his back. He listens when he is beaten."

At 12 or 14 it was time to marry and begin a family. For in the words of a New Kingdom scribe, "Take to yourselves a wife while you are young, so that she may give you a son. You should begat him for yourself when you are still young, and should live to see him become a man." And above all, "Make a holiday! And do not tire of playing!"

WRITE RIGHT

Egyptian students were required to learn three styles of writing. Each style had its place. Writing for everyday record keeping was a curly quick form of cursive lettering that ran right to left. Writing for tombs and monuments and all things everlasting was the cumbersome, time-consuming hieroglyphics. Between these two styles, a third type of writing that combined both forms was used for religious, scientific, and magical works. It ran from left to right. Late in ancient times a fourth style of script emerged for business use.

“ Traditional scribal advice, Papyrus Anastasi V, 1279–1212 BCE

“ New Kingdom scribal advice, "The Instructions of Ani," 1279–1212 BCE

“ Song of the Harpist, about 2040–1782 BCE

CHAPTER 18

<<RAMESSES II
ROYAL INSCRIPTIONS
AND HITTITE
EGYPTIAN PEACE
TREATY

WAR AND PEACE

RAMESSES II AND THE BATTLE OF QADESH

North of the Nile Delta, across the Mediterranean Sea, the land of the Hittites juts out like the snout of a barking dog. From an area where a whisker might sprout, the people of an initially insignificant nation called Hatti, began to spread throughout the Near East. By the late second millennium BCE, they had grown into a great power. Asian princes wrote time and again to Akhenaten, warning him that he had better stop the Hittites now, before it was too late. The Hittites were chipping away at Egypt's control in Syria. But Akhenaten ignored the letters and he ignored the Hittites. And the Hittites grew stronger.

In the 13th century BCE, during the early part of Egypt's 19th Dynasty, when Ramesses II was king, the Hittites could no longer be ignored. They controlled the city-state of Qadesh, and whoever controlled Qadesh controlled the trade route from the coast. It was a strategic position and Ramesses II knew it. "Now the vile enemy from Hatti had gathered together all the foreign lands as far as the end of the sea.... They covered the mountains and filled the valleys and were like locusts in their numbers." In the spring of his regnal Year 5, Ramesses II led his army eastward on a mission to beat back the Hittites.

<<Royal inscriptions, Qadesh battle inscriptions of Ramesses II, about 1279–1212 BCE

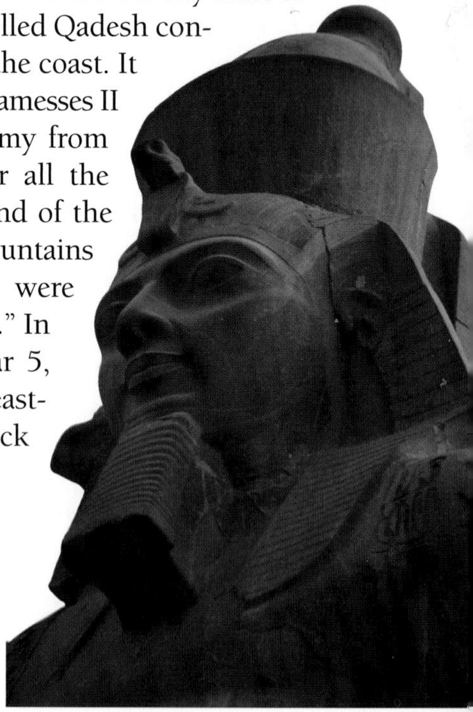

This close to Ramesses II's colossal statue, you can see the strings that hold the fake royal beard in place. Ramesses lived 96 years, kept 200 wives and concubines, and fathered more than 100 children.

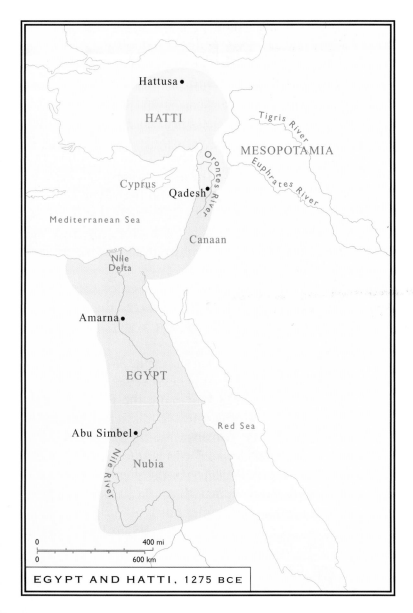

HATTI

Hattusa•

Tigris River

MESOPOTAMIA

Cyprus

Orontes River

Qadesh•

Euphrates River

Mediterranean Sea

Canaan

Nile Delta

Amarna•

EGYPT

Abu Simbel•

Red Sea

Nile River

Nubia

0   400 mi

0   600 km

EGYPT AND HATTI, 1275 BCE

LET MY PEOPLE GO

In the Biblical story of the Exodus, Moses petitions a pharaoh 10 times to allow him to lead the Hebrews out of Egypt. It is possible that the pharaoh was Ramesses II.

The Egyptian army was a fearsome force. Twenty thousand infantrymen and charioteers advanced toward Qadesh. Four divisions of highly trained soldiers, each unit named after a protective god—Amun, Re, Ptah, and Seth— marched east. Ox-drawn carts and donkeys loaded with food and weapons followed, kicking up dust as they went. Members of the royal family, priests, advisers, and diplo-

Soldiers adapted their weapons from farm tools. The curved double-edged sword looks similar to a scythe, which was used for cutting grain.

" Royal inscriptions, Qadesh battle inscriptions of Ramesses II, about 1279–1212 BCE

NOSE JOB

To keep the hook shape of Ramesses's nose from collapsing, embalmers stuffed his nostrils with peppercorns.

mats accompanied the soldiers to meet an enemy that Ramesses II claimed outnumbered them two to one.

Ramesses II and his faithful shield bearer, Menna, led the troops, riding front and center in a golden chariot. Tall and dignified, with flaming red hair and a prominent, hooked nose, the king looked exactly as a pharaoh should, heading out to vanquish his enemies. He indeed was Ramesses the Great.

The march through Canaan and southern Syria along the coastal road would take a month. It is likely that Ramesses had a timetable to meet. As was the custom, the time and place of the battle had probably been agreed upon. They were to arrive at Qadesh in May.

The city of Qadesh lay tucked into a crook formed by a fork in the Orontes River. A moat connected the two prongs of river, creating an island city. The water barrier made Qadesh easier to defend.

One day's march from Qadesh, in the Wood of Labwi, Ramesses and his men halted. They needed to rest before crossing the Orontes River and facing the Hittite army. A refreshed army was a strong army. While setting up camp, Egyptian sentries found two men hiding in the trees. The men claimed to have deserted the Hittite army and professed profusely their allegiance to the great and powerful Ramesses II. When questioned, they told Ramesses that the Hittite king had stalled 120 miles north of Qadesh. "He was too frightened to proceed southwards when he heard that the Pharaoh had come northwards."

Believing the story completely (flattery will get you everywhere) and without making any attempt to be sure it was true, Ramesses took one division, the Army of Amun, and crossed the river. The single division advanced quickly on Qadesh. The king anticipated an easy victory. Without the Hittite army there would be little opposition. Ramesses prepared for a sunrise surprise attack. But it was Ramesses who was in for the surprise.

That night the Egyptian patrol captured two Hittite spies. When they refused to talk, they were tortured and interrogated. "His Majesty asked, 'Who are you?' They replied, 'We belong to the king of Hatti. He has sent us to spy on you.' Then His Majesty said to them, 'Where is he the ruler of Hatti?' . . . They replied, 'Behold, the Ruler of Hatti has already come . . . They have their weapons of war at the ready. They are more numerous than the grains of sand on the beach. . . . ready for battle behind Old Qadesh.'"

Ramesses knew then that he had been tricked. The Hittite king and his entire army lay in wait just over the hill. And Ramesses' hasty advance had left his forces strung out on both sides of the river, miles apart. He was doomed. He called for his officers. Messengers were dispatched to summon the other field armies. The royal family was whisked away to safety.

Not yet knowing that the king and the Army of Amun were in mortal danger, the Army of Re approached the rendezvous point in a vulnerable formation. Their ranks stretched for two and a half miles. And they marched right into a trap. Hittite charioteers raced out from a line of trees and charged the Army of Re. The Egyptian soldiers panicked and scattered. Fleeing the battlefield, the soldiers led the enemy directly toward Ramesses II and the Army of Amun.

❝ Royal inscriptions, Qadesh battle inscriptions of Ramesses II, about 1279– 1212 BCE

DON'T BELIEVE EVERYTHING YOU READ

Ramesses wasn't a particularly skilled general. He was inexperienced, impatient, and gullible, but you would never know it from the inscriptions he commissioned. Some of the battle scenes, like Qadesh, are exaggerated accounts of true events. Others never happened at all and are merely symbolic images of what a great king should be—a super hero!

Details of the battle of Qadesh are carved on Ramesses II's mortuary temple. The Egyptian shield bearer holds his shield high to protect the fleeing soldiers from incoming arrows.

‟ Royal inscriptions, Qadesh battle inscriptions of Ramesses II, about 1279–1212 BCE

The first soldiers to reach Ramesses II's camp burst into the command tent, shouting that the Hittite army was right behind. Ramesses grabbed his battle armor and stepped out of the tent to see his camp already in chaos. The Hittites had broken through the defensive line. Ramesses realized he was isolated from his elite guards in the midst of the enemy with only his shield bearer, Menna, at his side. "When Menna saw so great a number of chariots had ringed about me, he felt faint, and fear entered his limbs. Thus he spoke to his majesty, 'We stand alone in the middle of the enemy. The infantry and the chariots have abandoned us. . . . Let us also leave unharmed.'" Ramesses stood firm and answered, "Steady your heart, Menna. I shall move among them just as a hawk."

The battle scenes carved on the walls of the Great Temple at Abu Simbel show Ramesses single-handedly taking down the Hittite army:

‟ Royal inscriptions, Qadesh battle inscriptions of Ramesses II, about 1279–1212 BCE

> There was no officer with me, no charioteer, no sol-
> dier. My infantry and my chariotry had run away
> before the enemy and no one stood firm to fight. . . .
> I found that my heart grew stout and my breast
> swelled with joy. Everything which I attempted I
> succeeded. . . . I found the enemy chariots scattering
> before my horses. Not one of them could fight me.
> Their hearts quaked with fear when they saw me and
> their arms went limp so they could not shoot. . . .
> I made them plunge into the water like crocodiles.
> They fell on their faces, one on top of another.
> I slaughtered them at will. . . . Behold, I am victorious,
> me alone!

What really happened when the Hittite army infiltrated the royal camp is muddied by Ramesses' illusions of grandeur. The camp surely was in mass confusion. Many of his soldiers undoubtedly deserted, fleeing for their lives. The Hittite army had a clear advantage. Their ambush had worked. But once they were inside the camp, things began to fall apart for the Hittites. Rather than pressing their advantage and fighting the Egyptians while they were most

vulnerable, the Hittites stopped to grab all the riches they were stumbling over. While they were busy plundering, Egyptian reinforcements arrived. The Egyptian divisions joined forces. They charged the Hittites. When it dawned on the Hittites that they were no longer facing disorganized stragglers, but a determined army, they turned and fled, diving into the Orontes River and swimming to the east bank where the bulk of the Hittite army waited.

When the dust settled, two of the greatest armies of the ancient world stood facing one another on opposite banks of the river. It seems neither wanted to fight. They had both lost many men. The Hittites no longer could ambush an unsuspecting army. The Egyptians would come at them prepared. And the Egyptians weren't facing some small outpost that offered little resistance. Hittite soldiers were trained and organized. War would mean enormous losses for both sides. And the outcome was by no means certain.

In a remote, sacred spot south of the Valley of the Kings, Ramesses II built his greatest monument, which Egyptians called "Place of Beauty" and we call Abu Simbel. Flanking the entrance of the Great Temple, carved into the limestone cliffs, are four giant statues of Ramesses II. The eyes, looking downward, watch those who approach six stories below.

Scribes recorded historical events that honored the king. Impressed onto this clay tablet is a copy of the treaty between Ramesses II and the Hittite king.

Royal inscriptions, Qadesh battle inscriptions of Ramesses II, about 1279–1212 BCE

Treaty between Hattusilis III and Ramesses II, 1258 BCE

Royal inscriptions, Qadesh battle inscriptions of Ramesses II, about 1279–1212 BCE

What happened next depends on whom you believe. Ramesses claimed the Hittite king begged for a truce by saying, "O victorious king, peace is better than war, Give us breath." The Hittite king claimed it was Ramesses who buckled under. The fact that Qadesh remained under Hittite control makes the Hittite king's version of the story more believable.

It took 16 years, but in Year 21 of Ramesses II's reign the two nations negotiated peace. The treaty is the earliest recorded document of its type preserved in its entirety. Inscribed on two matching silver tablets are the pledges of the king of Egypt and the king of Hatti to one another. "If a foreign enemy marches against the country of Hatti and if the king of Hatti sends me this message: 'Come to my help'... the king of the Egyptian country has to send his troops and his chariots to kill this enemy...." The Hittite king made a similar vow to defend Egypt. The treaty also pledged support if the enemy were to come from within. The Hittite king swore that if Ramesses should "rise in anger against his citizens after they have committed a wrong against him... the king of the country of Hatti, my brother, has to send his troops and his chariots...." Ramesses promised to stand by the Hittite king in the same circumstances. The treaty was honored until the fall of the Hittite Empire. Even when tested, Ramesses stood by his ally, announcing to the world, "Today there is a fraternity between the Great King of Egypt and the king of Hatti."

CHAPTER 19

SCRATCH AND SNIFF
VILLAGE LIFE

" EBERS PAPYRUS,
NOTES ON OSTRACA
AT DEIR EL-MEDINA,
AND OATH TAKEN
IN COURT

Flush toilets and trash pickups are *very* modern improvements. Did you ever wonder what life in a crowded place was like before these modern conveniences when people merely threw their waste out the door? The streets were so narrow in most ancient Egyptian villages that if you stretched out your arms, your fingertips would touch the buildings on opposite sides. So it didn't take long for these alleylike roadways to accumulate unhealthy amounts of trash. Imagine the stink of rotting garbage on top of human and animal excrement in the Egyptian heat. It's no wonder that everyone who could afford it burned incense in their homes. Better to catch a spicy whiff of frankincense and myrrh than the smelly stew piled onto the packed dirt streets.

The ground, baked rock-hard from the sun, was as solid as any modern poured-cement foundation. Brick makers carried mud from the Nile in leather buckets to the building site where it was mixed with straw and pebbles, then poured into wooden molds. The bricks dried quickly in the hot Egyptian sun. Unlike stone tombs and temples, mud-brick houses weren't meant to survive the homeowner. The bricks crumbled over time. If a house builder wanted to build a new house on top of a house that had collapsed, he merely watered the clay rubble. The soupy mix leveled itself like pudding in a pie plate and then hardened in the sun, making the perfect foundation.

Houses and additions were built willy-nilly. Most towns grew with no plan at all and expanded into a jumbled cluster of dwellings. Even towns that did have plans, such as Deir el-Medina, which was located across the river from

Living without air conditioning in a hot climate can be tough. Egyptians frequently slept on the flat roofs of their houses in order to take advantage of the cool night breezes.

TELL TALE

Archaeologists use the term "tells" for the mounds created from one settlement built over another settlement.

DONKEY BUSINESS

Many of the notes written on pieces of broken pottery found at Deir el-Medina were about donkeys. There were notes negotiating the trade of donkeys, the rental of donkeys, the lending of donkeys, and the borrowing of donkeys. There were even notes disputing rates for donkeys that died before the contract period ended. The going rate for donkey rental seems to have been 3¾ sacks of grain a month.

❝ Ebers Papyrus, about 1550 BCE

Thebes and used by the state for tomb builders and their families during the 13th century BCE, became chaotic after a while. Families added onto their houses where they could and divided the interiors to suit their personal needs.

The general layout of an Egyptian house was the same whether you were rich or poor—in fact, not just rich or poor, but also dead or alive, since tombs (and temples) followed the same design. If you were to visit a typical worker's home, you would pull aside the burlaplike cloth flap covering the doorway, which kept flies and dust out, and step into the entrance hall. There might be a sheep or donkey, pausing mid-chew to watch you pass though. Did a flea from the animal jump onto your head? Or did the flea jump off *you* onto the animal? In a hot, sandy environment fleas are a fact of life. Even though the Egyptians shaved their bodies from head to toe to keep the fleas and lice from having a place to hide, they were a constant problem. It must have been difficult to fall asleep with the fleas biting. The Ebers Papyrus had many housekeeping hints to keep scratching to a minimum and pests away. "To expel fleas in a house: sprinkle it throughout with natron water. To prevent mice from approaching: fat of cat is placed on all things. To prevent a serpent from coming out of its hole . . . a bulb of onion is placed in the opening of the hole and it will not come out."

The village of Deir el-Medina was home to well-paid tomb builders. Houses had real wooden doors and doorframes carved out of limestone, often inscribed with the home owner's name. The residents painted their doors red to repel demons. Beyond the entrance, you would enter a room for receiving guests. Egyptians owned very little furniture. You might sit on

The village of Deir el-Medina was home to the artists, scribes, stonecutters, and other craftsmen while they built the tombs in the Valley of the Kings.

a woven mat or perhaps a stool. Only the very wealthy had chairs. Homeowners placed statues of the gods into wall niches, but otherwise had none of the knickknacks modern families often like to collect. At Deir el-Medina one home-owner, concerned about leaving his valuables behind, took an inventory and asked that a house sitter watch over things while he was away. The letter gives us an idea of what a typical Deir el-Medina household might contain.

List of the items left behind by me in the village: [the words that are in italics are words we don't know the meaning of or how to translate them]

66 Notes on ostraca found at Deir el-Medina, about 1293–1070 BCE

- 3 sacks barley
- 1½ sacks emmer [grain]
- 26 bundles of onions
- 2 beds
- *sheqer*-box
- 2 couches for a man
- 2 folding stools
- 1 *pedes*-box
- 1 inlaid *tjay*-box
- *har*
- 2 griddle stones
- 1 *gatit*-box

- 2 footstools
- 2 folding stools of wood
- 1 sack lubya beans
- 12 bricks natron [salt]
- 2 tree trunks
- 1 door
- 2 *sterti* of sawn wood
- 2 *hetep*-containers
- 1 small *hetep*-container
- 1 mortar
- 2 *medjay*

...Please have Amen-em-wia stay in my house so he can watch it.

Bedrooms haven't changed much in thousands of years. It wouldn't be unusual to see toys strewn about children's rooms. Pillows, however, were quite different. Egyptians used headrests like the one under the bed frame.

Think about listing the entire contents of your house. Egyptians had far fewer belongings than we do today. The sacks of grain were the equivalent of cash. In a barter system you trade what you have for what you need. Do you need a donkey? Maybe your neighbor will trade for your bed.

Guests were never invited beyond the main room. The back of the house was private. Only the women, children, and immediate male members of the family were allowed there. It must have been a punishment, similar to making a child sit in the corner, to be sent to the back of the house. We know this because when Egyptians were trying to convince someone they were being sincere they would swear, "May I be sent to the back of the house if I am not telling the truth." So what was in the back of the house that was so awful? The kitchen was in the back of the house. At Deir el-Medina the kitchens were open air, with brick ovens in the shape of a beehive and stairs leading to the roof. Today getting sent to the kitchen isn't so bad. But in a hot desert climate, the room with the oven probably wasn't the most pleasant room in the house. In fact, the place in the house that seemed the nicest was the living space on the roof. Houses were dark and airless with no windows to bring in light or fresh air. Perhaps that's why the Egyptians often ate and slept on the roof.

The village of Deir el-Medina has been called a company town. The only people who lived there were the 40 to 60 tomb builders and their families. For generations the skilled craftsmen worked on the king's tombs, cutting into the cliffs of the west bank of the Nile across the river from the ancient city of Thebes. These artisans needed to be within easy commute of the **necropolis**, or city of the dead, where they worked. The workmen walked to the Valley of the Kings by way of a mountain path. During the week, rather than walking all the way back to their village, the workmen stayed at a camp of stone huts they had built on a level spot along the pathway. The tiny one- or two-room huts were clustered, sharing common walls. The group of huts looked like a honeycomb. An Egyptian workweek ran ten days, so it was not unusual for the workers to stay on the

66 Oath taken in court, court documents, about 1280 BCE

necro + *polis* = "dead" + "city"
A necropolis was quite literally a city for the dead. }

job for eight days and then travel to their families in the village for the "weekend."

Building a village within walking distance of the Valley of Kings had its problems. The biggest surely had to be water. Water had to be carried from the floodplain up to the valley to the village. With about 68 homes at Deir el-Medina, that's a lot of water. The state supplied half a dozen water carriers. And, of course, they recorded the deliveries. For the average six-person household, each person would get about four gallons a day for drinking and bathing (not including laundry, which was done by laundrymen, whose service was also provided by the state). Toting the water

Whether they lived in town or out in the country, Egyptians loved their gardens. They grew fruits and vegetables, and grape vines often climbed garden walls. Ramesses III said this about gardens: "I appointed gardeners from among the foreign captives to tend them and I dug pools of water for them filled with water lilies."

66 Notes on ostraca found at Deir el-Medina, about 1293–1070 BCE

must have been an annoyance, especially if the deliveries were delayed for any reason. But Deir el-Medina's misfortune turns out to be our good fortune.

To address the water problem, the villagers tried to dig a well. They dug, and they dug, and they dug. The well stretched 33 feet across and plummeted 170 feet down, with a descending spiral staircase cut into the rock wall. And still they never struck water. Finally, they gave up. The dry hole became a trash pit. The villagers filled it to the rim with, among other things, hundreds of records and letters written on pieces of broken pots—notes that give us a peek into the past. There are woeful letters from father to son ("I am wretched; I am searching for my sight but it is gone") and letters between lifelong friends ("since I was a child until today, I have been with you . . ."). There are shopping lists ("seek out for me one tunic in exchange for the ring; I will allow you ten days") and promises to do homework ("I will do it! See, I will do it, I will do it!"). Some things never change.

CHAPTER 20

BATTLE STATIONS
THE SEA PEOPLES

" INSCRIPTION FROM RAMESSES III'S MORTUARY TEMPLE AT MEDINET HABU

Ramesses III dispatched messengers. Advance squads of soldiers scrambled for the eastern Egyptian border. They raced to desert outposts and fortresses along the Delta, carrying an urgent message from their king. Hold your position. Stand firm. Keep the Egyptian border secure until the main army can be deployed. Reinforcements are coming. But until then, stay strong. Do not let the Sea Peoples past your line of defense.

By the end of the 13th century BCE, the Sea Peoples had swarmed across the eastern Mediterranean, burning and plundering everything in their path. They destroyed nearly every city, palace, town, and temple they came across. They had burned whole towns to ash and leveled cities to piles of rubble. Word reached Ramesses III that the Sea Peoples were on the move again, and this time it was Egypt they intended to crush. Ramesses III tells on the walls of his mortuary temple, "They were coming forward toward Egypt, while the flame was prepared before them."

Normally, the highly trained soldiers of the wealthiest country in the ancient world would not have been afraid of a disorderly crew of pirates, bandits, and ragamuffins. But the Egyptians believed this motley mob had already defeated the land of the Hittites and the island of Cyprus and that they were intent on conquering the world. The Sea Peoples had lost their homelands—had it been an earthquake that left them homeless? Or a drought that left them starving? Whatever drove them out had turned them into a dangerous

Egyptian artists had a stylized way to draw not only themselves, but also their enemies. This foreigner is shown with a beard—facial hair was considered to be the mark of a barbarian.

" Inscription from Ramesses III's mortuary temple at Medinet Habu, about 1174 BCE

enemy. They were desperate people who had nothing left to lose and everything to gain if they could force their way into Egypt.

Ramesses III's inscription tells us that he raced with his army toward southern Palestine to stop the Sea Peoples before they stepped on Egyptian soil. Every ship was sent to the mouth of the Nile, until Ramesses III had filled "the harbor-mouths, like a strong wall, with warships, galleys and barges." Ramesses III knew that he must draw a defensive line. The Egyptians believed this enemy had toppled empires. Egypt would not be one of them. He spared nothing outfitting his fleet. "They were manned completely from bow to stern with valiant warriors bearing their arms, soldiers of the choicest of Egypt..." Along the shore, Ramesses III positioned charioteers. "Their horses were quivering in their every limb, ready to crush the countries under their feet."

The Sea Peoples approached from the northeast. They came in waves. A vast horde advanced by land, a massive fleet bore down by sea—all headed straight for Egypt. Thou-

66 Inscription from Ramesses III's mortuary temple at Medinet Habu, about 1174 BCE

The Egyptian army marches on the wall of Ramesses III's main temple at Medinet Habu. Battle scenes on temple walls were most often real conflicts wildly exaggerated to make king and country appear invincible. Some battle scenes were complete fiction designed to prove the king's divine right to rule.

sands marched—young, old, families with wagons piled high with their belongings pulled by humpbacked oxen, soldiers in chariots, soldiers on foot—driven by the common goal of claiming Egypt's prosperous land for their own.

The first wave of Sea People attacked by land. From the scenes drawn at Ramesses III's mortuary temple, we see the chaotic mass of enemy soldiers as they launched themselves at the Egyptians. Some wore horned helmets. Others wore feathered helmets. Charioteers, three to a chariot, forced their horses into the fray. Swordsmen charged, slashing long, tapered swords. The infantry thrust their javelins and spears. Against them Ramesses III stood firm. King, chariot, and horses are shown in perfect alignment whereas the Sea Peoples are a chaotic jumble, facing slaughter, surrender, or flight. Ramesses III's troops fought with chins raised and lips pressed together in grim determination. The Sea Peoples scattered. Their soldiers turned and fled.

But now the battle moved to the Mediterranean. Egypt was not known for having much of a navy. Its navy was essentially the army with a little training at sea. Egyptians hated the sea—or the "Great Green" as they called it. Now they must fight the Sea Peoples on the Great Green.

From the text inscribed at Ramesses III's mortuary temple, we know that the Sea Peoples "penetrated the channels of the Nile Mouths" and that Ramesses III attacked "like a whirlwind against them." Although the Egyptian seamen were not as skilled as the Sea Peoples, their boats had oars—not just sails like the Sea Peoples' vessels. On open waters the Egyptian navy wouldn't have had a chance, but in the confined river mouths they could maneuver using oars. The Egyptian warships herded the Sea Peoples' boats closer and closer to land, where Ramesses III had lined the shore with archers. When the enemy ships were forced within firing range, the Egyptian archers let go volley after volley of arrows. The air filled with the hiss of their flight and the thwack of their landing. Egyptian marine archers joined the land archers firing from the boat decks in unison. Arrows fell like rain on the Sea Peoples who, armed with only swords and spears, cowered helplessly.

THEME PARK

Ramesses III's mortuary temple is like a theme park. And the theme is Ramesses III's victory in battle. Even the architecture more closely resembles a fortress than a temple. To enter, a visitor must first pass guardhouses in front of the entrance. A thick, mud-brick wall surrounds and protects the whole complex. The temple's outer walls show Ramesses III vanquishing his enemies. Recorded on a pylon and the northern exterior wall are the details of his victory over the Sea Peoples.

Inscription from Ramesses III's mortuary temple at Medinet Habu, about 1174 BCE

MEANWHILE IN THE AEGEAN...

The Mycenaean and Minoan civilizations collapsed at about this time, perhaps at the hands of the very same Sea Peoples.

MYSTERY OF THE SEA PEOPLES

The Sea Peoples changed the ancient world dramatically. Despite their profound impact on history, who they were, where they came from, what drove them out, and where they finally ended up remains a mystery to this day.

Pictures of Ramesses III killing prisoners are carved on the walls of one of his temples. Depictions of the king's conquests, displayed where everyone could see them, were used to boost the king's image as a powerful leader.

📖 Inscription from Ramesses III's mortuary temple at Medinet Habu, about 1174 BCE

📖 Inscription from Ramesses III's mortuary temple at Medinet Habu, about 1174 BCE

The Egyptian seamen used their oars to maneuver the warships even closer. They tossed grappling hooks into the Sea Peoples' vessels. When the hooks took hold the Egyptians heaved on the lines and capsized the Sea Peoples' boats. As they tumbled into the water they were "butchered and their corpses hacked up." Others were grabbed, chained, and taken prisoner before they could swim to shore.

In the victory scene at the mortuary temple, we see a pile of severed hands presented to Ramesses III. Prisoners taken alive were branded and assigned to labor forces. The vizier counted everything—hands, spoils, prisoners—for an official report. *Ma'at* had conquered chaos. The battle against the Sea Peoples had been won. "Their hearts and their souls are finished for all eternity. Their weapons are scattered in the sea."

CHAPTER 21

HAPPILY EVER AFTER
THE ARTS

Rules, rules, rules...we may think that rules and creativity don't go together, but for the Egyptians, art was all about rules. Are you painting the king? Make sure you don't draw anything in front of his face or body. That was not a trick shot the king was making with the bow flexed behind his back. The painter was just obeying the rule. When sculpting people seated, make sure that their hands rest on their knees. Always draw the important people bigger. Follow the rules.

Walk into any art museum anywhere in the world and you will be able to pick out the Egyptian art immediately. The rules created a style that lasted with almost no change for 3,000 years. The style is called frontalism. Egyptian artists drew the head in profile and the body straight on. By drawing figures with these angles, artists could show a large number of body parts—both arms, both legs, the nose. The Egyptians believed that the drawings could come to life and journey to the afterlife. It's nice to go to eternity with as much of your body as possible.

Unlike modern painters who try to give their paintings depth, Egyptian painters made everything look flat. Two artists often worked on the same painting. One artist drew the outline. During the Middle Kingdom, these artists were called "scribes of outlines." And the second artist,

One of the most popular themes in Egyptian literature, music, and art is the importance of pleasing the gods. This unfinished tomb painting is a typical day in the afterlife, with Egyptians bringing gifts to the god Anubis.

known as a "colorist," painted in the color as if he were working on a coloring book. Do you think he was told to "stay within the lines"?

Artists almost never signed their work. The art was not about the artist. Artists were not innovators, they were craftsmen, and as you can tell from their Middle Kingdom titles, they were more closely related to scribes than to the "artist" types we think of today. That's not to say Egyptian artists weren't talented. One sculptor created two life-size sculptures of a high priest and his princess wife that were so realistic they scared off tomb robbers. The stone eyes implanted in the statues appeared to watch the thieves, and frightened them so badly that they dropped their tools and ran.

Perhaps what contributed to the tomb robbers' fear was the Egyptian belief that art had magic. Often you will see crocodiles, hippos, and snakes drawn with spears sticking out of them. If a crocodile suddenly came to life right next to you, you would probably appreciate the spear. And since these murals were one day going to become a reality, it's nice that the banquet scene has plates piled high with delicious food.

It must have been the attention to rules that led Egyptian artists to discover the "sacred ratio." The proportions in the sacred ratio repeat throughout the natural world. Plants, flowers, and trees grow in the sacred ratio. Sunflowers, pinecones, and the nautilus shell spiral according to the sacred ratio. The earth and the moon measure, and the galaxies spin—all to this sacred proportion. Egyptian artists drew the human body according to the sacred ratio, in the same way modern artists do today.

Egyptian art students learned the fundamentals of the sacred ratio by first drawing a grid that turned the work surface into a graph. They then could apply the proportions to almost anything—jewelry, hieroglyphs, pyramids, and architecture. The sacred ratio was so important to Egyptians they believed that tombs not following the proportions prevented the deceased from going to the afterlife and temples not built according to the rules would displease the gods. Pleasing mathematical proportions in art and architecture are not the only thing moderns have borrowed and built on

EVERYBODY LOVES PHI

The golden ratio for rectangles is when the ratio of length to width equals 1.6180339.... This number is called "phi" (not to be confused with "pi" which is another ratio altogether—a circle's circumference to its diameter). "Phi" is named after the Greek sculptor, Phidias, who used this pleasing ratio in his work. One of the first examples of the golden ratio is thought to be the Great Pyramid of Giza.

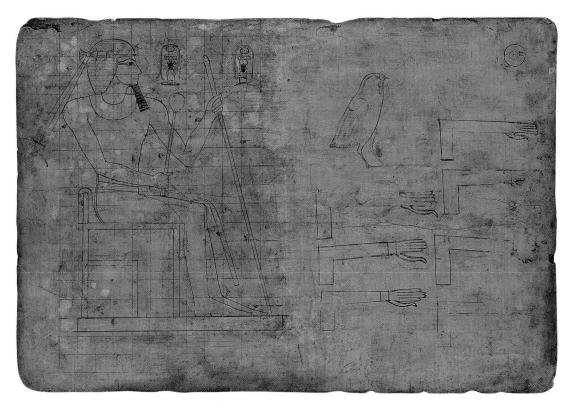

from the ancient Egyptians. Many of our modern tales have their roots in Egyptian literature. Do you recognize parts of this story?

Once upon a time there was a young maiden named Rhodopis who was kidnapped by pirates and sold to a kind, old Egyptian. The old man spent his days sleeping under a tree, so he didn't know that the other servant girls in his house were mean to Rhodopis.

"Rhodopis, fetch the wood. Weed the garden, Rhodopis. Clean the stable. Wash the clothes. Mend my robe, Rhodopis." The chores continued from dawn to dusk. The servant girl's only friends were the animals. When she washed the clothes at the riverbank, Hippopotamus slid up the mud incline to be near her. When she weeded the garden, Monkey climbed down the tree to sit by her side. And at the end of the day, Rhodopis sang and danced for her animal friends.

It is not surprising that Rhodopis enjoyed music. Tombs and temple walls are covered with images of dancers and

A drawing board shows the grid-marked figure of Thutmose III. The ancient unit of measure called a cubit is based on the distance between the elbow and fingertips. The cubit is divided into palm widths: four fingers measured across the knuckles. Artists used grid lines and cubits to draw figures in perfect proportion.

❝ Egyptian story of Cinderella retold by Strabo, about 63 BCE–21 CE

musicians. There were percussion instruments—drums, cymbals, and tambourines. There were wind instruments—flutes and trumpets. And there were stringed instruments—harps, lyres, and lutes. Everyone enjoyed music, from the pharaoh to the field worker. No one loved a festival more than the Egyptians. Crowds sang and clapped along with the musicians who paraded through the streets. Dancers performed for the revelers, moving with the grace of gymnasts—cartwheeling, twirling, flipping. and gyrating to the rhythm. Music and dance were integral to Egyptian daily life. Workers labored to the beat, priests praised the gods in music and motion. Musicians and dancers entertained at banquets and ushered the dead at funerals. So, for a young servant girl to sing to the animals at day's end is not surprising at all.

Rhodopis twirled so lightly her feet barely grazed the ground. Unknown to Rhodopis, she was dancing near the tree where the old man slept and her movement woke him. He was so taken by her grace that he decided right then and there that her feet should have the finest shoes in the kingdom. "He ordered her a special pair of slippers. The shoes were gilded with rose-red gold and the soles were leather.

66 Egyptian story of Cinderella retold by Strabo, about 63 BCE–21 CE

In this ancient jam session, a singer snaps his fingers to the flutist's beat. Flutes are older than the pyramids, but some ancient song lyrics still sound modern. This New Kingdom chorus from the Harris Papyrus went: "Have a good time. Do not grow tired of it. Look, there is nobody allowed to take his property with him. Look, there is nobody who is gone and returns."

Now the servant girls really disliked her for they were jealous of her beautiful slippers."

News traveled to their village that the king was having a party. The entire kingdom was invited. On the day of the party the servant girls put on their finest clothes. They gave Rhodopis a long list of chores and handed her mounds of laundry to be washed in the river. They laughed at her washing the clothes as they poled down the river to the king's banquet.

Hippopotamus accidentally splattered the beautiful slippers. Rhodopis cleaned them carefully and put them in the sun to dry. "As she was continuing with her chores, the sky darkened and as she looked up, she saw a falcon sweep down, snatch one of her slippers, and fly away." Could that be the god Horus who had taken her shoe? Rhodopis put the one slipper into her tunic and returned to her chores.

At the banquet the king was staring out at the crowd. He was thinking he would much rather be out hunting in the desert than hosting a party when "suddenly the falcon swooped down and dropped the rose-red golden slipper in his lap." Knowing this was a sign from Horus, the king "sent out a decree that all maidens in Egypt must try on the slipper, and the owner of the slipper would be his queen."

As you may have now guessed, the king traveled his kingdom by chariot searching high and low. Maidens everywhere tried to squash their wrong-sized feet into the slipper. Then he took to the Nile on his royal barge and one day he docked near the home of Rhodopis. The servant girls who tormented Rhodopis recognized the slipper at once but said nothing. One after another they tried to cram their feet into the golden slipper and one after another they failed. The king saw Rhodopis hiding in the rushes and asked her to come forward and take her turn at the slipper. "She slid her tiny foot into the slipper and then pulled the other from her tunic."

And as if it were a golden rule . . . the king and Rhodopis lived happily ever after.

TUT'S TOOTER

One of the items King Tutankhamen thought worthy of bringing to the afterlife was a trumpet. The more than 3,300-year-old silver trumpet found in his tomb has been played twice. The first time it shattered. After it was restored, it was played one more time in 1939 and recorded by BBC Radio.

> Egyptian story of Cinderella retold by Strabo, about 63 BCE– 21 CE

> Egyptian story of Cinderella retold by Strabo, about 63 BCE– 21 CE

CHAPTER 22

KING FOR A DAY

KUSH, NUBIA, AND THE THIRD INTERMEDIATE PERIOD

A ROSE BY ANY OTHER NAME

Ethiopia is the Greek word for Nubia. It means "Land of the Burnt Faces." People who live close to the equator have darker skin than those who live farther away. The Nubians lived closer to the equator than the Egyptians. The Greeks called them *Ethiopes* or "Burnt-Faced Ones." To the Greeks, Ethiopia was the area that is now northern Sudan and the Upper Nile Basin. In the Old Testament Nubia is called Kush. In the New Testament, which was written in Greek, Nubia is called Ethiopia.

If you had asked Egyptians 3,000 years ago for directions to Nubia, they would have looked at you quizzically. Huh? Nubia? What's that? It would be more than 1,000 years (about 20 CE) before the Greek geographer Strabo named the area in southern Egypt and northern Sudan "Nubia," after the nomadic people, the Nuba, who roamed there. Before that the Egyptians called it *Ta-Seti*, which means "The Land of the Bow," because its archers were so skilled. But the ancients knew it as the Kingdom of Kush. During the Middle Kingdom, Kush was not much more than a southern outpost of Egypt, but gold can change even the most rugged land. And Kush had gold mines. By the first millennium BCE, Kush had grown into a country strong enough to save a troubled Egypt. And Egypt was in trouble again. It was entering another intermediate period—a time without strong central kingship.

King Piye of Kush must have shaken his head sadly as he watched Egypt break up into small clumps of power. There was very little violence among the different groups (King Piye did not like bloodshed), so that wasn't what was bothering Piye. It was the weakening of Egypt that worried him. Four centuries earlier, at the end of the New Kingdom, the Two Lands had indeed split into *two* lands.

The priests of Amun at the temple of Karnak in Thebes became so powerful that they ruled Upper Egypt (which is the southern part of the country). The pharaoh held on as best he could to Lower Egypt (which is the northern part of the country). In its weakened state, Egypt was vulnerable. We know from *The Tale of Wenamun* that Egypt had lost respect in the ancient world. The story makes it clear that Egypt no longer made foreign rulers tremble.

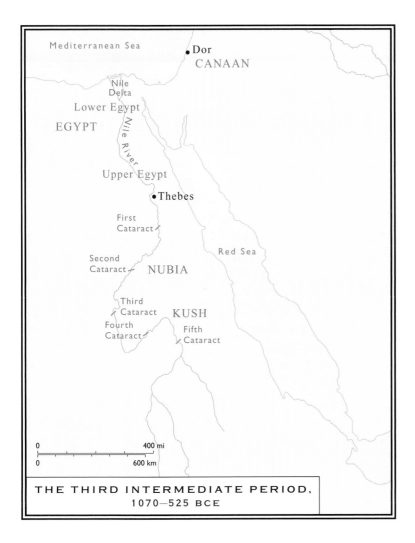

Mediterranean Sea

• Dor

CANAAN

Nile
Delta

Lower Egypt

EGYPT

Nile River

Upper Egypt

• Thebes

First
Cataract

Red Sea

Second
Cataract

NUBIA

Third
Cataract

KUSH

Fourth
Cataract

Fifth
Cataract

| 0 | | 400 mi |
| 0 | | 600 km |

THE THIRD INTERMEDIATE PERIOD, 1070–525 BCE

The high priests of the temple Karnak sent the priest Wenamun on a journey "to fetch timber." Wenamun was to trade silver and gold for wood needed to build a ship for the god Amun—a ship he would use to sail across the sky. Not long after he left Egypt, Wenamun was robbed. The silver and gold disappeared in Dor, on the coast of what is now Israel. Wenamun complained to the King of Dor, "I have been robbed in your harbor. But you are the prince of this land and you are its controller. Search for my money, for indeed the money belongs to Amun, King of the Gods." Wenamun warned the king that he was Amun's ambassador.

66 *The Tale of Wenamun,* about 1070 BCE

The statue of Amun traveled from temple to temple in a sacred boat carried by priests. When Amun— in the form of his statue—was inside the temples, only priests had access to him, but during festivals he was available to everyone.

When the thieves robbed Wenamun, they robbed Amun as well. And anyone stealing from Amun was stealing from Egypt. The king of Dor didn't seem worried. In fact, he practically accused Wenamun of lying. He said, "Are you in earnest or are you inventing? For indeed I know nothing of this tale that you have told me." When Egypt was at the peak of its power, the King of Dor would have raced to right the wrong, fearful of Egypt's revenge, but now he treated Wenamun with contempt. Egypt had lost its grip.

The Third Intermediate Period was just the first chapter in what would be 1,000 years of foreign rule. Egypt was conquered again and again and again, first by the Libyans, then by the Nubians, Persians, Greeks, and finally the Romans. Scholars are having a horrible time trying to sort out who was king when. The dynasties no longer represented one king taking the throne at the death of another. Now kingships overlapped, with every major community claiming that its prince was the legitimate heir to the throne. It must have been all the quarreling that drove King Piye in Kush to take action.

Shortly after he took the throne of Kush, in the middle of the eighth century BCE, King Piye sent his sister north to take control of Upper Egypt. Kush had a close connection with the priests of Amun at Karnak because of a rock. Not just any rock, but an outcropping on a mountaintop shaped like the head of a cobra. The cobra was the Egyptian sym-

PRINCESS, ANYONE?

Another sign of Egypt's decline was the sudden willingness to marry off Egyptian princesses. There was a time when pharaohs wouldn't consider marrying off their daughters to foreign rulers. In the 10th century BCE, Solomon, the king of Israel, married the daughter of an Egyptian king, breaking that tradition.

bol for royalty. This isolated mountain rose out of the plain about a mile from the Nile, and Egyptian priests had built a temple at the base of it. To the priests of Amun the "Holy Mountain" was the most important place of worship outside of Karnak. To the Kushites it was proof from Amun himself that they were the rightful heirs to the throne of Egypt. King Piye appointed his sister, "The Divine Wife of the God." She became the high priestess and mortal goddess at Karnak. As wife of Amun, she ruled Upper Egypt.

Lower Egypt was divided into several separate and independent kingdoms that didn't agree on much, but one thing they did agree on was that Kushite control of Upper Egypt was not acceptable. Something had to be done about it. Four Northern "kings" joined together and planned a rebellion.

You can almost hear King Piye's loud sigh. He'd have to go north himself to put an end to the uprising. He didn't see the advance as an invasion; he saw it as a rescue. It was his duty to restore *ma'at* to Egypt. He was honor bound to reunite the Two Lands, quiet the internal conflict, and reestablish Egypt as a world power once again, just as pharaohs before him had been divinely driven to do. He took the name *Sema-tawy*, meaning "Uniter of Two Lands," and rallied his army. "Yoke the war horses, the best of the stable; draw up the line of battle!" Inscribed on a six-foot, square block of pink granite are the details of Piye's "rescue."

King Piye sent forces north to battle the coalition of four kings, instructing his men to go quickly and press on, but when they arrived at Thebes and the temple of Karnak, they were to purify themselves. Piye told them, "you shall enter the water, you shall bathe in the river, you shall dress in fine linen, unstring the bow, loosen the arrow." Karnak was Amun's temple, after all, and since Amun had sent them, they must pay their respects.

Grim and determined, Piye's army marched north. On the Nile "they found many ships coming upstream bearing soldiers, sailors, and commanders, every valiant man of the Northland, equipped with weapons of war." The army from Kush crushed them. They "made a great slaughter. . . . [Egyptian] troops and their ships were captured. . . ." The

CARING FOR WEAPONS

If soldiers were not using their bows, the bows had to be unstrung or the taut bowstring would stretch and quickly become useless. It took two men to string a soldier's bow.

Stela of Piye, about 747–716 BCE

Stela of Piye, about 747–716 BCE

Stela of Piye, about 747–716 BCE

This scene painted on the front panel of a chest is symbolic of the king triumphant over the forces of chaos. Here the larger-than-life hero stands alone defending Egypt against the Nubians.

two enemies clashed on land as well as on water. Kushite soldiers chased the armies of Egypt and slayed them in their own neighborhoods, laying siege to cities and sending captives back to Kush. And still they pushed northward, doing battle as they went.

King Piye wanted to join his army, but first he had to keep his promise to attend the Festival of Opet. No king of Egypt could afford to ignore the rituals of the Opet Festival because they confirmed a king's right to rule. If Piye expected the people to accept him as the divine king of Egypt, his place was at Karnak. This was the most important festival of the year. For the farmers whose fields were flooded, and had little to do until the waters receded, the festival was a month-long street party, with food and music and carefree days. For the king, it had a more serious side.

During the second month of the flood season, the great god Amun (well, actually just the god's statue, but that was basically the same thing to the Egyptians) left his sanctuary at Karnak and spent a month in southern Opet, which is modern-day Luxor. *Opet* means "secret chamber." The secret rooms deep in the temple at Luxor were believed to sit on the mound of creation, the holiest of places. Every year Amun would travel the mile from Karnak to the shrines

there. It was the only time Amun left his temple at Karnak.

The priests of Karnak carried Amun—in the form of his statue sitting in his sacred boat—on their shoulders in a parade through the streets. The procession was led by high priests wearing panther-skin capes, burning resin, scattering sand, and waving fans. A man in front played the tambourine. Until the late New Kingdom the priests carried the boat the entire way to the temple at Luxor, but by Piye's time the journey was made by river. The priests placed Amun, still in his sacred boat, in the center of an elaborately decorated barge waiting on the Nile. The gold used to decorate the barge alone weighed four and a half tons. Getting the barge to move was no easy task. An army of men grabbed ropes tied to the barge. To the beat of tambourines, songs, and trumpets' blare, they dragged the floating temple. Both banks of the river were lined with spectators shouting encouragement. Along the procession route Egyptians slaughtered and cooked oxen, baked bread, and served fruit to the crowds. While they feasted, they were entertained by musicians, dancers, and acrobats. It was a 28-day party, lasting until Amun traveled back to Thebes and disappeared into the depths of the temple of Karnak to be taken care of by priests.

Piye threatened his enemies that on the day Amun returned to Karnak, he planned to "make the Northland taste the taste of my fingers." Ancient threats lose a little in the translation, but that must have been a very fierce oath because "every heart was heavy with fear of him." Piye laid siege to towns and used battering rams against their walls. He built a tower "to elevate the archers while shooting, and the slingers while slinging stones." And when it was over, and Piye had succeeded, he inscribed on his "victory stela,"

PRIESTS HOLD THE PURSE STRINGS

From the Middle Kingdom on, the highest positions at the temple of Karnak were passed down from father to son rather than appointed by the king. As the priests became more powerful and more independent, they established their own dynasties, controlling Upper Egypt and claiming to be Egypt's protector. The Amun priesthood owned two-thirds of all the land in Egypt belonging to temples, along with 90 percent of all ships and 80 percent of all businesses. The priests had a tight hold on Egypt's economy.

Stela of Piye, about 747–716 BCE

66 Stela of Piye, about 747–
716 BCE

**PYRAMIDS
POPPING UP**

Piye was the first king to
build pyramids in Kush.
Piye's uncle, who followed
Piye to the throne, loved to
build pyramids so much
that Kush ended up having
more pyramids than Egypt.

as the Stela of Piye is known, what bothered him more than
anything else "It is more grievous in my heart that my horses have suffered hunger, than any evil deed...." The stela
shows Piye was a compassionate man. He forgave his enemies, treating the now defeated kings with generosity by
appointing them governors of their lands.

King Piye had no desire to remain in Egypt. Kush was
his home. He had fulfilled his holy obligation to Amun and
reunited the Two Lands. Now he could return to the kingdom of Kush and rule from there. When he died he was
buried in his homeland just north of the Holy Mountain.
His pyramid was modest, with an underground chamber at
the base of a stairway. In a nearby tomb his love for his horses is clear. There, standing and facing east, his team of four
chariot horses waits, ready to journey with their master to
the afterlife.

*Model soldiers are ready to join their general in the afterlife. The general's tomb contained two wooden
models of 40-men units, a group of Egyptian spearmen, and this model of Nubian archers.*

CHAPTER 23

GREAT EXPECTATIONS
THE GREEK PERIOD

Children growing up in the fourth century BCE in a country called Macedon, just north of Greece, loved adventure stories. A favorite of the king's young son was a long poem by Homer about the Trojan War called the *Iliad*. Young Alexander read it so often he had parts of it memorized. The hero he liked best was the warrior Achilles. Alexander dreamed that one day he'd be just like him— bold and brave, nearly invincible. Alexander's mother used to whisper in his ear that he was a descendant of Achilles, that Alexander was destined to do great things. His mother wasn't the only person pushing Alexander. His teacher, Aristotle, encouraged him, too. Aristotle wrote notes in the margins of a copy of the *Iliad* and gave it as a present to Alexander. Alexander couldn't wait to grow up and accomplish great things!

When Alexander was still a young boy, not even in his teens, a horse breeder brought a magnificent black stallion with a white blaze across its forehead to sell to the king. The terrified animal reared, pawing the air, screaming. No one could calm the animal. According to the Greek biographer Plutarch, the horse "turned fiercely on the grooms." The king lost patience with the unmanageable horse and ordered the breeder to take it away. Alexander was so upset he called out, "What a horse they are losing, for want or skill and spirit to manage him!" Irritated, the king snapped at his son, "Young man, you find fault with your elders, as if you knew more than they, or could manage the horse better." But Alexander was not about to give up, and boldly told them all, "I certainly could." The horse breeder and grooms laughed at Alexander. This *boy* thinks he can do better than the king's best horsemen. But the laughter died away when Alexander "ran to the horse, and laying hold on the bridle, turned him to the sun."

The Egyptian people crowned Alexander the Great pharaoh and gave him the throne name Mery-Amun Setepen-Re, which means "Beloved of Amun, Chosen by Re." Although Alexander spent only six months in Egypt, he changed Egypt more than any other pharaoh.

66 Plutarch, *Life of Alexander*, about 79 CE

Plutarch, *Life of Alexander*, about 79 CE

Back when the grooms were struggling to control the stallion, Alexander had noticed that the horse's wild eyes were fixed on its shadow jerking this way and that beneath its feet. With the stallion's shadow now behind him, Alexander "kept speaking to him softly and stroking him." Then, to everyone's astonishment, Alexander threw off his cloak and leaped onto the stallion's back. There was no laughter now. Everyone held their breath as Alexander galloped across the open plain, then led the stallion back to where they stood. The king, finally finding his voice, said, "Seek another kingdom, my son, that may be worthy of your abilities; for Macedonia is too small for you."

It wouldn't be long before Alexander did just that. Riding his stallion, who carried him into every major battle for the next two decades, and carrying his copy of the *Iliad*, which he kept along with a dagger under his pillow each night, Alexander set out to conquer the world.

It was a much older and war-weary Alexander who marched into Egypt. He had been king since his father's assassination in 336 BCE. Not only did the 20-year-old Alexander rule Macedon, but he also ruled the country his father had conquered as well—Greece. For someone who had grown up being told that he was destined for greatness, just "holding on" to what his father had won in war was not nearly enough. Alexander attacked the Persian Empire, gaining ground in bloody battle after bloody battle, just like his hero Achilles.

Alexander's mother still whispered in his ear. Her stories grew more and more like the ravings of a mad woman. She claimed that Alexander's real father was *not* the mortal king of Macedon, but Zeus, the king of the gods. Zeus had come to his mother in the form of a snake and produced Alexander. Alexander knew his mother slept with snakes. Could one of them have been the mighty Zeus? Could Zeus be his real father?

In late October of 332 BCE, Alexander pushed his army across the desert and into Egypt. While his fleet sailed south to Memphis, Alexander led his troops by land. The soldiers marched past gleaming white temples. Flanked by columns,

IT'S ALL GREEK TO ME

From Alexander's favorite poet, Homer, we get the word "Hellenism." It began as the name used to describe a tribe of Greeks led by Chief Hellen. But now it is used to describe anyone associated with Greece around the time of Alexander the Great. Greek rule in Egypt lasted three centuries, from when Alexander the Great "conquered" Egypt to the death of Cleopatra VII.

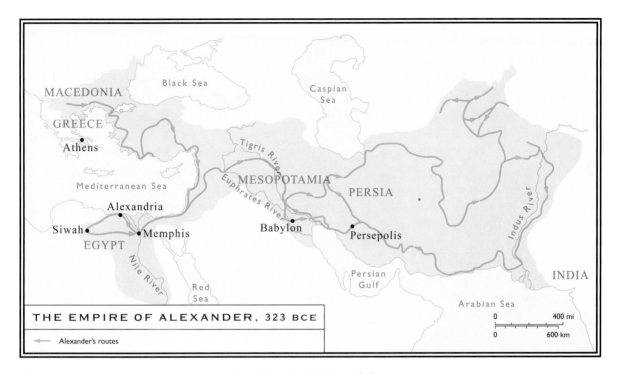

THE EMPIRE OF ALEXANDER, 323 BCE

←— Alexander's routes

the entrances were so enormous that they looked as if they had been built for giants. Alexander and his men had never seen anything built to this scale. Just when Alexander thought nothing could possibly beat the grandeur of these homes of the gods, he came to the great pyramids of Giza. White limestone ramps rose from a perfectly level plain to heights no one dreamed possible. Here was a land that lived by the gods and died by the gods. For Alexander, who was deeply religious, nothing could have been more uplifting. He marched into Memphis, and instead of resistance, he was met by crowds of cheering Egyptians, frenzied with joy.

The Egyptians were happy to see Alexander because Egypt had been occupied for almost 200 years by Persia. The Persians had taxed the Egyptians heavily and drained the grain reserves. The Egyptians could probably have tolerated every hardship—except one. The Persians made the fatal mistake of not respecting Egypt's gods and traditions. The Persians destroyed temples, ridiculed beliefs, and butchered sacred bulls. Alexander was their savior, their liberator, and soon to be their new king.

IT'S A WONDER

Limestone casing blocks once covered the outside of the Great Pyramid. The pyramids are so mind boggling that they made it onto a rather elite list. They are one of the Seven Wonders of the Ancient World—the only wonder still standing, and the oldest.

Even the Romans were fascinated by the stories told about Alexander and his battles against the Persians. When Mt. Vesuvius erupted and covered the town of Pompeii, this mosaic was buried for nearly 2,000 years.

On November 14, 332 BCE, in Memphis, Alexander was crowned pharaoh and the double crown of the Two Lands was placed upon his head. The high priest carried out the coronation according to the 3,000-year-old tradition. Alexander was named "son of the gods." This was not his mother whispering in his ear, this was a country—a whole country—declaring that he was divine. The Greeks carefully kept their gods and their people separate. But here, in Eygpt, Alexander was finding the line between the two was quite fuzzy, especially when it came to the pharaoh.

Alexander worshipped Amun as an Egyptian representation of Zeus. He dutifully offered sacrifices to the sacred bull that the Persians had butchered and he ordered the temples rebuilt. Overjoyed, the Egyptians engraved Alexander's image on monuments all over Egypt.

For two months Alexander studied at the royal palace in Memphis. He studied the Egyptians' philosophy, law, and religion. He read their stories. He paid tribute to their gods. Even though Alexander loved to read and to study, for a man who got his thrills on the back of a horse swishing a sword at his enemies, two months of sitting still is a long time. So in January, Alexander set out again to follow his dream—literally to follow his dream. The Greek biographer Plutarch writes that Alexander

> chanced one night in his sleep to see a wonderful vision; a grey-headed old man . . . appeared to stand by him, and pronounce these verses:
>
> An island lies, where loud the billows roar,
> Pharos they call it, on the Egyptian shore.

66 Plutarch, *Life of Alexander*, about 79 CE

The man at his side in his dream was none other than his favorite author, Homer. Pharos was a place Alexander knew from another long poem written by Homer, the *Odyssey*. "Out of the sea where it breaks on the shores of Egypt rises an island from the waters: the name men give it is Pharos." If this place were as fabulous as Homer claimed, Alexander would build a city there—a port city to service his empire.

66 Homer, *Odyssey*, about 750 BCE

When Alexander got to Pharos, he was delighted. Standing on the shoreline across from the island, Alexander noticed that arcs of land sheltered the natural harbor from sea storms. Cool breezes fanned the shoreline. The Greek author Arrian writes that Alexander "was immediately struck by the excellence of the site, and convinced that if a city were built upon it, it would certainly prosper. Such was his enthusiasm that he could not wait to begin the work and himself designed the general layout of the town, indicating the position of the market place and the temples."

66 Arrian, *Anabasis of Alexander*, about 130 BCE

Grabbing fistfuls of chalk dust, Alexander paced off the perimeter of the city with long strides, marking the outline in white. Behind him breathless architects and surveyors raced to keep up. The docks for the harbor should go here—Alexander would have pointed out—right across from the island in his dream. This city would be in the same shape as their military cloaks, and angled to take advantage of the sea breeze. Alexander ran out of chalk dust before he ran out of ideas. He had plans for underground drains and sewers, a palace, forts, temples, shrines... more chalk! His attendants came running with baskets of barley flour. Alexander scooped out handfuls, outlining the market square, the city walls, when suddenly Alexander came to a screeching halt. Flocks of hungry gulls were eating his city plan! Horrified, the group watched. In a flash it was gone—all gone. Was this an omen? Was Alexander's port city destined to doom? Alexander's seer collected himself first. No, no, he reassured Alexander. This was a *good* sign. It meant the city would be so rich in all things it would "be the nurse and feeder of many nations."

Suddenly, Alexander was struck by an overwhelming desire to seek out an oracle. Oracles knew the words of the gods, and in ancient times no major decision was made without first checking what the oracle had to say about it. The Greek oracles tended to be much more talkative than the Egyptian oracles. Greek oracles predicted the future. Egyptian oracles were much more tight lipped. They stuck to yes or no answers about whether the gods were pleased or (gulp) not. The oracle whom Alexander had a sudden urge to visit was Greek and in the Siwah Oasis. The heroes in the stories Alexander had read in his boyhood traveled to this particular place, and now Alexander wanted to follow in their footsteps. There was only one problem: 300 miles of hostile desert lay between Alexander and the shrine of Ammon at Siwah Oasis.

Alexander headed southwest from the coastline toward central Africa. He followed an ancient caravan route that wound its way from oasis to oasis like a connect-the-dots puzzle. One of those dots was Siwah. Alexander would discover that the desert is a dangerous, unforgiving place. Four days' journey from the nearest oasis, their water supplies ran out. The unrelenting sun beat down on Alexander and his men. They would not survive the four days in the heat. Perhaps many had given up all hope and were making peace with their gods when the skies opened up and the rain pelted them, filling their water containers and soaking the men. Surely this was a sign from the gods that

❝ Plutarch, *Life of Alexander*, about 79 CE

YOU SAY AMMON, I SAY AMUN

Ammon is what the first Greeks to visit the Siwah Oasis called their god, a poor translation of Amun. But it fits. The Greek word for "sand" is *ammos*.

Alexander was a favored son, meant to live on and continue to do great things?

Did they begin to doubt again when the hot south winds began to blow? The wind whipped itself into a fury, sweeping sand, blinding the guides, shifting the dunes, and wiping out all signs of the trail. The guides were lost. Was Alexander destined to wander aimlessly through the desert until he and his men dropped and were picked apart by vultures? Alexander did not have doubts, even if his men did. Plutarch writes that Alexander had been so lucky in life that it "made his resolve unshakable and so he was able to overcome not only his enemies, but even places and seasons of the year." And lucky he was, or as he would have preferred to believe—saved by the gods. Because just then, two black ravens miraculously flew in, squawking as if to say, "This way. Siwah is this way."

Although migrating birds stop along their way at Siwah, it makes for a much more interesting legend if Alexander used supernatural powers to summon the ravens. Everyone traveling with Alexander was sure that he had. And now there were some who thought maybe he was the son of Zeus after all. Perhaps no one was surer than Alexander himself. And when the Egyptian high priests at the temple at Siwah greeted Alexander with rusty Greek, meaning to say, "Oh, my son," but instead mispronounced it and said, "Oh, son of god," Alexander was quite pleased. All that was left was for the oracle to confirm it.

No one knows what Alexander asked the oracle deep inside the inner recesses of the temple. When he came back out into the daylight, he refused to say. In a letter to his mother he wrote that he would tell her when he returned home. But the secret went to his grave with him. Alexander died before he could see his mother again. Alexander the Great left Egypt in April of 331 BCE. He would never see Egypt again either—at least not alive. Ten years later he was buried in the city he had laid out with chalk dust and barley flour, a city he named after himself: Alexandria.

66 Plutarch, *Life of Alexander*, about 79 CE

In about 130 BCE, the historian Arrian described the shrine of Ammon at the Siwah Oasis as "surrounded on all sides by the waterless desert of sand; but in the midst of this waste there is a small plot of ground five miles wide at its broadest point, and thickly planted with fruit trees—olives and date-palms." Alexander was the first pharaoh to make the dangerous journey to Siwah.

CHAPTER 24

" LETTER OF
ARISTEAS, PLINY
THE ELDER,
INSCRIPTION
ON THE PHAROS
LIGHTHOUSE,
PLUTARCH,
SHAKESPEARE,
PTOLEMY, AND
HERON

THE LAST CHAPTER
GRAECO-ROMAN RULE

" *Letter of Aristeas*, about third
century BCE

**BCE (BEFORE
COMPUTERS EXISTED)**

Much of the Old Testament
would be lost but for works
diligently copied by hand
in the rooms of the Library
of Alexandria.

Alexander the Great died without an heir. His kingdom
was divided among his generals. General Ptolemy got
Egypt. Ptolemy's Macedonian descendants ruled Egypt for
three centuries until Cleopatra VII died by snake. Egypt
lost its independence and became a province of the Roman
Empire around 30 BCE. The End.

Or was it?

You could go to the library and check. It's too bad you
can't go to the library in Alexandria during the time of the
Ptolemies. That was some library. General Ptolemy was a
writer, and like most writers he loved books. But nothing
can compare to the obsession for collecting of his son,
Ptolemy II. From a letter probably written some time in the
third century BCE, we see the magnitude of the Ptolemy
family's ambition: "keeper of the king's library, received
large grants of public money with a view to his collecting,
if possible, all the books in the world." Imagine trying to
collect them *all*!

Ptolemy II sent agents to every corner of the world to
buy up libraries. He sent letters to prominent people beg-
ging to borrow their books so he could copy them. Ships
anchoring in the harbor at Alexandria were immediately
boarded and searched by the police. The police weren't
looking for smugglers. They were looking for books. If they
found any, they were confiscated and taken to Ptolemy II,
who had them copied. The *copies* were returned to the ships
and the *originals* were taken to the Library. Ptolemy II had
no shame when it came to the library. He put down a
deposit to "borrow" great works from Athens and then kept
them, sending back copies and forfeiting the deposit. The
Athenians were not happy. Imagine borrowing Shakespeare's plays written in his own hand, then keeping the
originals and returning a photocopy.

By the time Cleopatra VII ruled 200 years later, the Library may have housed 700,000 scrolls, rolled around dowels and stored on its shelves, available to anyone who could read and longed to learn. Keeping track of all these great works was no easy task. It took the skills of fine librarians. The poet Homer's editor was the first librarian. He concentrated on acquiring as many books as he could. The second head librarian organized them. He created a system that grouped the works by subject. Eratosthenes took over after that. Eratosthenes was an all-around scholar who dabbled in this and dabbled in that. His two favorite subjects were geography and mathematics. He accurately measured the earth's diameter by comparing the shadows in Alexandria to those in Aswan at noon on the same day of the year. Using the lengths of the shadows and the distance between the two cities, he was able to calculate the diameter of the earth. Methods that Eratosthenes developed are still used by mathematicians today. The end for Egypt? Hardly.

Alexander the Great's seer was on the mark when he predicted that Alexandria would one day feed the world. Alexandria grew under the Ptolemies into the largest, richest city on earth. Compared to Alexandria's white marbled majesty, Rome was a dirty, foul-smelling slum. Alexandria attracted intellectuals, merchants, and tourists. It was a bustling city where the voices of Egyptians, Greeks, Arabs, Syrians, Judaeans, Persians, Nubians, Phoenicians, Italians, and Gauls could be heard. Its harbor might hold 1,000 ships on any given day. And guiding them through the narrow, rocky entrance was a beacon that shined from what would become one of the Seven Wonders of the

MEANWHILE IN ASIA MINOR...

The second largest library in the ancient world was in Pergamum in Asia Minor. The word "parchment" comes from "Pergamum." Parchment was invented when King Ptolemy refused to export papyrus to Pergamum. Parchment isn't yellowed brittle paper, but untanned animal skins (think of the skin we stretch over drums). It was more durable than papyrus, could be written on both sides, and folded without damage. The Pergamum Library was eventually given as a gift to Cleopatra from Mark Antony.

The lighthouse of Alexandria looks more like a modern skyscraper than a working lighthouse. The lighthouse was a tourist attraction, complete with food vendors on the observation deck. There was also a small balcony near the top for anyone willing to make the climb for the view.

Ancient World—the Pharos Lighthouse—built on the very island that first summoned Alexander the Great in a dream.

The lighthouse built during the time of Ptolemy II was second only to the Great Pyramid as the tallest building on earth. At the top was a curved mirror of polished metal that reflected the flames of a fire, sending a guiding light to ships at sea. Writing much later, in the first century CE, historian Pliny the Elder tells us, "The only danger is, that when the fires are thus kept burning without intermission, they may be mistaken for stars, the flames having very much that appearance at a distance." This is still a problem with lighthouses—at sea, their lights just above the horizon look like stars.

❝ Pliny the Elder, *Natural History*, first century CE

When the lighthouse was completed, the architect Sostrates wanted to carve his name in the foundation. But Ptolemy II refused. Ptolemy II wanted only one name on the lighthouse—his. But a man who could design something so fabulous that it would one day become a Wonder could surely come up with a clever solution. And he did. Sostrates chiseled his name into the stone foundation and then plastered it over. He chiseled Ptolemy II's name into the plaster. Years later, after both were dead and gone, the plaster cracked, crumbled, and fell away, revealing: "Sostratus, the son of Dexiphanes, the Cnidian, dedicated this to the Saviour Gods, on behalf of those who sail the seas."

❝ Inscription on the Pharos Lighthouse, third century BCE

Although earthquakes tumbled the lighthouse 1,600 years later, its legacy lives on. Today lighthouses are modeled after the Lighthouse of Alexandria, and *pharos* is the root for the word "lighthouse" in French, Italian, and Spanish. No end here, either.

All the Ptolemies loved learning and building. But the Ptolemies also lusted for power and would do anything to get it and keep it—cheat, steal, lie, even kill. When Ptolemy XII felt his power slipping, he made a deal with Rome. Egypt had grain. Rome had might. Ptolemy XII promised an entire year of Egypt's crops if Rome would use its military power to keep him on the throne. When the Egyptians learned that Ptolemy XII had sold them out, putting them deep into debt, they chased him off the throne and right out of the country.

With Ptolemy XII gone, it appeared as if his oldest daughter would become the next pharaoh. But she "mysteriously died." Some say her younger sister, Berenice, ordered the killing. Berenice, like the rest of the Ptolemies, was certainly cold-blooded enough to order the execution. We know that she had her husband strangled three days after they were married, just because he bored her.

While Berenice established herself on the throne, Ptolemy XII hid out in Rome. He convinced the Romans that if they wanted their grain, they would have a better chance collecting from a king sitting on the throne, rather than a king in exile, so the Romans used their military might to put Ptolemy XII back in business. One of Ptolemy XII's first commands upon his return was to have his daughter Berenice killed. No one knew better than a Ptolemy how dangerous it was to allow someone with designs on the throne to live.

Ptolemy XII made it clear in his will that his next daughter, Cleopatra VII, along with his son, were to take his place ruling Egypt after his death. He must have trusted Cleopatra (who was known as "She Who Loves Her Father") not to speed up his trip to the afterlife.

When her father died in 51 BCE (from natural causes), Cleopatra was 18 years old. She was a young woman full of ambition. She ignored the fact that she was supposed to share the throne with her younger brother and took on the role of pharaoh with gusto. Although Cleopatra was a Ptolemy through and through, and would not hesitate to remove the competition, she also was blessed with an extra dose of the Ptolemies good qualities. She was the only one of her entire family (the first in nine generations) to learn Egyptian. She could communicate with her 8 million subjects in their own language. In fact, she could communicate with her enemies, too. The historian Plutarch tells us, "she could easily turn to whatever language she wished, so that she very seldom needed an interpreter."

Although modern movies like to present Cleopatra as an extraordinary beauty, Plutarch tells us that she wasn't particularly attractive; she wouldn't "strike those who looked

RACIAL TENSION

Not all was rosy in Alexandria. Cultural clashes flared in the streets of Alexandria. Like-minded Alexandrians—from wealthy merchants to servants—formed the Alexandrian Mob and took it upon themselves to dole out "justice." The Mob grew so powerful that even kings feared it—with good reason, as King Ptolemy XI found out. Forced to marry his stepmother whom he detested and who was much older than he, Ptolemy solved his "problem" by murdering her just 19 days after they married. Big mistake—the Mob loved her. They snatched Ptolemy XI right out of the palace, dragged him into the street, and killed him.

Plutarch, *Life of Antony*, 110 CE

Plutarch, *Life of Antony*, 110 CE

GRAND ENTRANCES

Cleopatra's best-known entrance is when she met Caesar in 48 BCE. One night, Caesar's guards announced that a merchant was waiting outside with a gift for Caesar. The man entered Caesar's quarters with a carpet slung over his shoulder. When he unrolled it, Cleopatra tumbled out.

at her; but her companionship was irresistible and spellbinding." Friend and enemy alike, she made sure she knew their language and everything else about them. She knew that it was Egypt's wealth that interested Rome. So she went to great length to show off Egypt (and herself) as wealthier than the Romans could possibly imagine. When she escorted the Roman ruler Julius Caesar on a journey up the Nile, it was aboard a royal barge built like a floating palace, complete with gardens and columned walkways. Cleopatra and Caesar sailed the length of Egypt. They drifted past temples, the great pyramids, the Sphinx, and the true source of Egypt's fortune: mile after mile of golden fields of wheat and barley.

After Caesar's death, Cleopatra welcomed one more Roman statesman and general—Mark Antony—onto another boat. This royal ship had been carefully staged to ooze

Even this scene from the 1934 movie Cleopatra *couldn't outdo the real Cleopatra's over-the-top entrances. When she first met Mark Antony, she was dressed as the goddess Venus, sailing in a golden ship with purple sails and silver oars.*

opulence. She ordered the ship painted gold, the sails dyed purple, the oars crafted from silver. Women, draped in gauzy fabric that fluttered in the breeze, steered the ship, while the silver oars dipped to the tempo of lute and pipe music. Under a canopy woven from gold threads, fanned by boys dressed as cupids, Cleopatra reclined on a couch. The perfume-drenched sails announced her arrival on the wind. Shakespeare writes that the sails were, "so perfumed that/ The winds were lovesick with them" and that "From the barge/A strange invisible perfume hits the sense/Of the adjacent wharfs." Cleopatra knew how to make an entrance. When she finally welcomed Antony aboard, he had to make his way across a floor covered in a foot and a half of rose petals.

Cleopatra didn't just use Egypt's wealth to entice the Romans to help her build an empire. She, as many of the Ptolemies before her, valued knowledge as much as power. One of her favorite projects was expanding the "Museum" in Alexandria—the temple dedicated to the gods of arts and sciences, the Muses. The Museum was an ancient version of today's think tanks. The greatest minds of the times gathered at the Museum to study, exchange ideas, and publish. They studied physics, literature, medicine, astronomy, geography, philosophy, mathematics, biology, and engineering.

Scholars were exempt from paying taxes, and the government provided their living expenses, which left them free to roam the Museum thinking great thoughts. And what a beautiful place to ponder! The Museum overlooked the harbor's crystal blue water. There were fountains and botanical gardens and zoos with exotic animals. There was even an observatory above the dining room for stargazing. No wonder great thinkers were drawn to Alexandria.

Imagine wandering into a classroom where Archimedes, one of the three greatest mathematicians of all time, was giving a lecture. He lived much of his life at the Museum.

Portraits of Cleopatra on coins give us a clue as to what she looked like. There are no surviving full-length statues and few written descriptions. Those who met Cleopatra came away enchanted. Historian Dio Cassius said she was "brilliant to look upon and listen to…" and Plutarch called her "irresistible" and "bewitching."

" Shakespeare, *Antony and Cleopatra*, 1606 CE

AROMATHERAPY

Cleopatra knew that no one loved roses more than the ancient Romans. Rose petals littered tables and floors at banquets; public fountains and baths spewed rosewater; people stuffed their pillows with rose petals, ate rose pudding, and wore roses around their necks and in their hair. At banquets in the first century CE, Nero had pipes installed under the dinner plates to spray the guests between courses with rosewater. At one of his banquets a guest smothered to death under a blanket of rose petals.

ALEXANDRIA'S HONOR ROLL

Euclid (325–265 BCE)	*Greek mathematician; Euclidean geometry is named for him*
Callimachus (300–240 BCE)	*Second librarian of the library at Alexandria; referred to as the "Founding Father of Librarians"*
Archimedes (287–212 BCE)	*Mathematician and inventor from Syracuse, Sicily*
Eratosthenes (276–194 BCE)	*Third librarian of the library at Alexandria; his works still provide a basis for modern scientific methods*
Julius Caesar (100–44 BCE)	*Roman ruler; his soldiers may have inadvertently set fire to the library*
Heron (10–75 CE)	*Greek mathematician; published the first book on robots and on other mechanical devices that worked by air, steam, or water pressure*
Ptolemy (Second century CE)	*Greek astronomer and geographer; wrote a 13-volume work,* Almagest, *about mathematical and astronomical systems; not related to the Ptolemaic kings of Egypt*

Who would guess that someone living 2,200 years ago would be working on calculus and physics? In the math wing you might just stumble into Euclid. At some point you will take geometry, and you can blame Euclid for that. He wrote *Elements* at the Museum. *Elements* has been used as a math textbook longer than any other. Mathematicians still study Euclidean geometry today.

If math is not your thing, you could wander down to the dissecting rooms. Cleopatra did. Students dissected goats, pigs, monkeys—even humans. They learned that arteries did not carry air, as everyone had thought, but blood, and that the heart pumped it. They studied anatomy firsthand, learning the purpose of the heart, the kidneys, the brain. One physician advised his students training to become doctors, "look at the human skeleton with your own eyes. This

Galen, medical writings, mid-second century CE

is very easy in Alexandria...the physicians of that area instruct their pupils with the aid of autopsy." That physician later went into sports medicine and landed a job as physician to the gladiators.

Maybe the thought of cutting up bodies makes you squeamish. Then the class for you might be mechanics taught by Heron. He published the first book on robots (yes, nearly 2,000 years ago!), which describes more than 100 machines, including one that is very similar to a jet engine. He entertained his students by using toys to teach

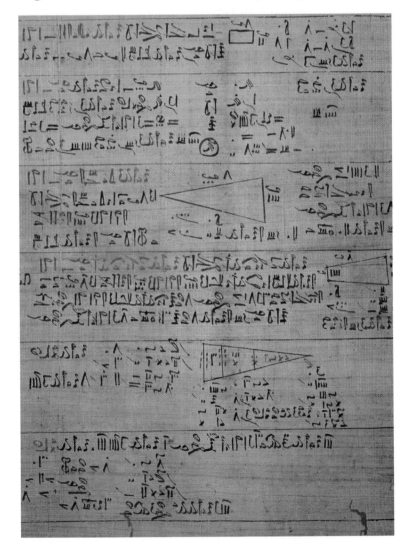

The Ahmes mathematical papyrus, named after the scribe who copied it around 1650 BCE, looks a lot like math homework. The papyrus contains math tables and more than 80 problems and their solutions.

Heron, *Pneumatica*, about second or third century CE

them physics. In his classroom your lessons would be "singing birds and sounding trumpets, puppets that move when a fire is lit on an altar, animals that drink when they are offered water…" He built statues that sang—from compressed air. His class was a gas.

Wander into the great scientist Ptolemy's lecture. An astronomer and geographer, he wrote a book (13 volumes) about the movements of the sun, moon, and planets. For 15 centuries that textbook was the springboard for all star study. It only took eight volumes for Ptolemy to map the known world according to longitudes and latitudes. Until Ptolemy the maps were very inaccurate, with the Roman Empire appearing to hog most of the planet. Ptolemy's mind was a stellar wanderer. He wrote in the opening of one of his books,

Ptolemy, *Almagest*, second century CE

> Well do I know that I am mortal, a creature of one day.
> But if my mind follows the winding paths of the stars
> Then my feet no longer rest on earth, but standing by Zeus himself I take my fill of ambrosia, the divine dish.

Come to think of it, there is no need to wander into their classrooms. They've wandered into yours. From your maps to your math, there is something in every school that began in Alexandria more than 2,000 years ago. These were thinkers ahead of their time. One thousand eight hundred years before the astronomer Copernicus, Aristarcus of Samos proved that the earth revolved around the sun, not the other way around. One thousand eight hundred years before Columbus, Eratosthenes proved the earth was round. Two thousand two hundred years before Melvil Dewey, Callimachus created a subject catalogue to keep track of the scrolls in the Library at the Museum. And *that's* just the beginning….

TIMELINE

The centuries BCE and CE are mirror images of each other. The years go backwards before the year 1 CE. So someone born in 2000 BCE who died in 1935 BCE would have lived to be 65 years old. On both sides of the "mirror," the 200s can also be called the 3rd century, the 900s are called the 10th century, and so on— BCE as well as CE.

BCE

About 3200
Writing begins in Egypt

3150
King Scorpion rules during Dynasty 0

3100
Narmer/Menes unifies Egypt

3050
Early Dynastic period (Dynasties 1–2) begins; Aha rules as first king of Dynasty 1

2700
Old Kingdom period (Dynasties 3–6) begins

2668–2649
Djoser rules, builds first pyramid

2600–2500
Pyramid Age (construction of three major pyramids at Giza) begins

2589–2566
Khufu (Cheops) rules, builds Great Pyramid at Giza

2558–2532
Khafre (Chephren) rules, builds Second Pyramid and the Sphinx at Giza

2532–2504
Menkaure (Mycerinus) rules, builds Third Pyramid at Giza

2278–2184
Pepi II rules; Dynasty 6 comes to an end

About 2180
First Intermediate Period (Dynasties 7–10) begins; time of general unrest

2040
Middle Kingdom period (Dynasties 11–12) begins

1991–1962
Amenemhet I, first king during Dynasty 12, rules

1971–1926
Senwosert I, second king during Dynasty 12, also known as Senusret I, rules

1782
Hyksos invade; Second Intermediate Period (Dynasties 13–17) begins

1573–1570
Last king of Dynasty 17 rules

1570
Hyksos are expelled; New Kingdom period (Dynasties 18–20) begins

1570–1293
Dynasty 18

1500–1483
(Queen) Hatshepsut rules as Pharaoh, sends trading expedition to Punt

1483–1450
Thutmose III succeeds stepmother Hatshepsut, becomes Pharaoh of Egypt

1483
Thutmose III leads Egypt in Battle of Megiddo and defeats rebels

1386–1349
Amenhotep III rules, initiates "Golden Age" of Egypt with far-flung international contacts and foreign trade

1350–1334
Akhenaten and Nefertiti rule Egypt and create religious upheaval and "heresy" (possible beginnings of monotheism)

1334–1325
Tutankhamen, the "boy king," rules Egypt briefly, before dying of unknown causes

1293–1185
Dynasty 19

1279–1212
Ramesses II rules Egypt

1274
Ramesses II fights Hittites in Battle of Qadesh to a tie

1207
First attack of the Sea Peoples

1185–1070
Dynasty 20

1182–1151
Ramesses III rules Egypt

1174
Ramesses III defeats the Sea Peoples

1069
Third Intermediate Period
(Dynasties 21–26) begins

747
Nubian/Kushite Dynasty (Dynasty 25)
begins; Piye rules Kush and then Egypt as
the first king of Dynasty 25

525
Persia conquers Egypt; Late Period
(Dynasties 27–31) begins

332
Alexander the
Great invades; the
Hellenistic Period
in Egypt and the
Near East begins

305
Ptolemaic
Dynasty begins
in Egypt

3rd century
Manetho, Egyptian priest and historian,
first divides Egypt's history and pharaohs
into dynasties

305–282
Ptolemy I, Greek general under Alexander
the Great, rules Egypt as the first of the
Ptolemaic Macedonian dynasty

285–246
Ptolemy II is second ruler of Egypt during
the Macedonian dynasty; great Lighthouse
(Pharos) at Alexandria, one of the Seven
Wonders of the Ancient World, is built

246–222
Ptolemy III, third ruler of Egypt during
the Macedonian dynasty, establishes the
great Library at Alexandria

205–180
Ptolemy V, fifth ruler of Egypt during the
Macedonian dynasty is best known for the
Rosetta Stone, which was inscribed and
displayed during his reign

196
Rosetta Stone inscribed, in hieroglyphs,
demotic, and Greek, during reign of
Ptolemy V

51–30
Cleopatra VII rules Egypt as the last of the
Ptolemaic dynasty

30
Cleopatra dies; Hellenistic Period ends;
Roman rule begins in Egypt

FURTHER READING

Entries with 📖 *indicate primary source material.*

GENERAL WORKS ON ANCIENT EGYPT

Bagnall, Roger S. *Egypt in Late Antiquity.* Princeton: Princeton University Press, 1993.

Baker, Rosalie, and Charles F. Baker III. *Ancient Egyptians: People of the Pyramids.* New York: Oxford University Press, 2001.

Bowman, Alan K. *Egypt After the Pharaohs, 332 BC–AD 642: From Alexander to the Arab Conquest.* 2nd ed. Berkeley: University of California Press, 1996.

Brewer, Douglas J., and Emily Teeter. *Egypt and the Egyptians.* Cambridge: Cambridge University Press, 1999.

Broida, Marian. *Ancient Egyptians and Their Neighbors: An Activity Guide.* Chicago: Chicago Review Press, 1999.

Chauveau, Michel. *Egypt in the Age of Cleopatra: History and Society Under the Ptolemies,* Trans. David Lorton. Ithaca, N.Y.: Cornell University Press, 2000.

Clayton, Peter A. *Chronicle of the Pharaohs: The Reign-By-Reign Record of the Rulers and Dynasties of Ancient Egypt.* London: Thames and Hudson, 1994.

Gardiner, Sir Alan. *Egypt of the Pharaohs.* London: Oxford University Press, 1961.

Hawass, Zahi A. *Secrets from the Sand: My Search for Egypt's Past.* New York: Abrams, 2003.

Hoffman, Michael A. *Egypt Before the Pharaohs.* New York: Knopf, 1984.

Kemp, Barry J. *Ancient Egypt, Anatomy of a Civilization.* London: Routledge, 1991.

Lewis, Naphtali. *Life in Egypt Under Roman Rule.* Oxford: Clarendon Press, 1993.

Midant-Reynes, Beatrix. *The Prehistory of Egypt: From the First Egyptians to the First Pharaohs.* Oxford: Blackwell, 2000.

Payne, Elizabeth, and J. Thomas. *Pharaohs of Ancient Egypt.* New York: Random House, 1964.

Roberts, Russell. *Rulers of Ancient Egypt.* San Diego: Lucent, 1999.

Shaw, Ian, ed. *The Oxford History of Ancient Egypt.* Oxford: Oxford University Press, 2002.

Silverman, David P., ed. *Ancient Egypt.* New York: Oxford University Press, 1997.

Trigger, Bruce, et al. *Ancient Egypt, a Social History.* Cambridge: Cambridge University Press, 1983.

Wilson, John. *The Culture of Ancient Egypt.* Chicago: University of Chicago Press, 1951.

ATLASES

Baines, John, and John Malek. *Atlas of Ancient Egypt.* New York: Facts on File, 1980.

Haywood, John. *World Atlas of the Past, Vol. 1: The Ancient World.* New York: Oxford University Press, 1999.

DICTIONARIES AND ENCYCLOPEDIAS

Arnold, Dieter. *The Encyclopedia of Ancient Egyptian Architecture.* Princeton, N.J.: Princeton University Press, 2003.

Redford, Donald, ed. *The Oxford Encyclopedia of Ancient Egypt.* 3 vols. New York: Oxford University Press, 2001.

Vernus, Pascal, and Jean Yoyotte. *The Book of the Pharaohs.* David Lorton, trans. Ithaca, N.Y.: Cornell University Press, 2003.

BIOGRAPHY

Baker, Rosalie F. and Charles F. *Ancient Egyptians: People of the Pyramids.* New York: Oxford University Press, 2001.

Fox, Robin Lane. *Alexander the Great.* New York: Penguin, 1994.

AKHENATEN AND NEFERTITI

Aldred, Cyril. *Akhenaten: King of Egypt.* London: Thames and Hudson, 1988.

Arnold, Dorothea. *The Royal Women of Amarna: Images of Beauty from Ancient Egypt.* New York: Metropolitan Museum of Art, 1996.

Freed, Rita E., and Sue D'Auria. *Pharaohs of the Sun: Akhenaten, Nefertiti, Tutankhamen.* Boston: Museum of Fine Arts in association with Bulfinch Press/ Little, Brown and Co., 1999.

Redford, Donald B. *Akhenaten: The Heretic King.* Princeton, N.J.: Princeton University Press, 1984.

Reeves, Nicholas. *Akhenaten: Egypt's False Prophet.* London: Thames and Hudson, 2001.

Tyldesley, Joyce A. *Nefertiti: Egypt's Sun Queen.* New York: Viking Press, 1999.

AMENHOTEP III

Fletcher, Joann. *Chronicle of a Pharaoh: The Intimate Life of Amenhotep III.* New York: Oxford University Press, 2000.

Kozloff, Arielle P. and Betsy M. Bryan. *Egypt's Dazzling Sun: Amenhotep III and His World.* Cleveland, Ohio: Cleveland Museum of Art, 1992.

O'Connor, David, and Eric H. Cline. *Amenhotep III: Perspectives on His Reign.* Ann Arbor: University of Michigan Press, 1998.

CLEOPATRA

Brooks, Polly Schoyer. *Cleopatra: Goddess of Egypt, Enemy of Rome.* New York: HarperCollins, 1999.

Grant, Michael. *Cleopatra.* London: Phoenix Press. 2000.

Hughes-Hallet, Lucy. *Cleopatra: Histories, Dreams and Distortions.* New York: HarperCollins, 1991.

Stanley, Diane. *Cleopatra.* New York: HarperTrophy, 1997.

Walker, Susan. *Cleopatra of Egypt: From History to Myth.* Princeton, N.J.: Princeton University Press, 2001.

HATSHEPSUT

Andronik, Catherine M. *Hatshepsut, His Majesty, Herself.* New York: Atheneum, 2001.

Carter, Dorothy Sharp. *His Majesty, Queen Hatsheput.* New York: HarperCollins, 1987.

Tyldesley, Joyce A. *Hatchepsut: The Female Pharaoh.* New York: Viking Press, 1996.

RAMESSES II

Kitchen, Kenneth A. *Pharaoh Triumphant: The Life and Times of Ramesses II.* Warminster: Aris & Phillips, 1982.

Tyldesley, Joyce A. *Ramesses: Egypt's Greatest Pharaoh.* New York: Penguin, 2001.

KING TUT (TUTANKHAMEN)

Brier, Bob. *The Murder of Tutankhamen: A True Story.* New York: Berkeley, 1999.

Donnelly, Judy, and James Watling. *King Tut's Mummy... Lost and Found.* New York: Scholastic, 1988.

Reeves, Nicholas. *The Complete Tutankhamun.* London: Thames and Hudson, 1990.

ART, ARCHITECTURE, AND MUSIC

Bourriau, Janine. *Pharaohs and Mortals: Egyptian Art in the Middle Kingdom.* Cambridge: Cambridge University Press, 1989.

Clarke, Somers, and R. Engelbach. *Ancient Egyptian Construction and Architecture.* New York: Dover Publications, 1990.

Doxiadis, Euphrosyne. *The Mysterious Fayum Portraits: Faces from Ancient Egypt.* New York: Abrams, 1995.

Manniche, Lise. *Music and Musicians in Ancient Egypt.* Reprint, New York: Dover Publications, 1992.

———. *Musical Instruments from the Tomb of Tutankhamen.* Oxford: David Brown Book Co., 1976.

Robins, Gay. *The Art of Ancient Egypt.* Cambridge, Mass.: Harvard University Press, 1997.

Walker, Susan. *Ancient Faces: Mummy Portraits in Roman Egypt.* Boston: Routledge, 2000.

Wilkinson, Richard H. *The Complete Temples of Ancient Egypt.* London: Thames and Hudson, 2000.

———. *Reading Egyptian Art: A Hieroglyphic Guide to Ancient Egyptian Painting and Sculpture.* London: Thames and Hudson, 1992.

———. *Symbol & Magic in Egyptian Art.* London: Thames and Hudson, 1999.

CHILDREN, SCHOOL, AND GAMES

Decker, Wolfgang. *Sports and Games of Ancient Egypt,* trans. Allen Guttmann. New Haven: Yale University Press, 1992.

Janssen, Rosalind M., and Jac J. Janssen, *Growing Up in Ancient Egypt.* London: Rubicon Press, 1996.

Piccione, Peter A. *Senet, Gaming With the Gods: The Game of Senet and Ancient Egyptian Religious Beliefs.* Leiden: Brill Academic Publishers, 2004.

Wroble, Lisa A. *Kids in Ancient Egypt.* New York: Rosen, 2003.

DAILY LIFE

Kaplan, Leslie C. *Home Life in Ancient Egypt.* New York: Powerkids Press, 2004.

McDowell, Andrea G. *Village Life in Ancient Egypt: Laundry Lists and Love Songs.* New York: Oxford University Press, 2002.

Meskell, Lynn. *Private Life in New Kingdom Egypt.* Princeton, N.J.: Princeton University Press, 2002.

Romer, John. *Ancient Lives: Daily Life in Egypt of the Pharaohs.* New York: Holt, Rinehart and Winston, 1984.

Ross, Stewart. *Ancient Egypt: Family Life.* London: Hodder & Stoughton, 2001.

HIEROGLYPHS

Collier, Mark, and Bill Manley. *How to Read Egyptian Hieroglyphs: A Step-By-Step Guide to Teach Yourself.* Berkeley: University of California Press, 1998.

Donoughue, Carol. *The Mystery of the Hieroglyphs: The Story of the Rosetta Stone and the Race to Decipher Egyptian Hieroglyphs.* New York: Oxford University Press, 1999.

Giblin, James Cross. *The Riddle of the Rosetta Stone: Key to Ancient Egypt.* New York: HarperCollins, 1990.

McDermott, Bridget. *Decoding Egyptian Hieroglyphs: How to Read the Secret Language of the Pharaohs.* San Francisco: Chronicle Books, 2001.

Parkinson, Richard B. *Cracking Codes: The Rosetta Stone and Decipherment.* Berkeley: University of California Press, 1999.

Zauzich, Karl-Theodor. *Hieroglyphs Without Mystery: An Introduction to Ancient Egyptian Writing,* trans. Ann Macy Roth. Austin: University of Texas Press, 1992.

KUSH, MEROE, AND NUBIA

Hayes, Joyce. *Nubia: Ancient Kingdoms of Africa*. Boston: MFA Publications/Museum of Fine Arts, 1994.

Morkot, Robert G. *The Black Pharaohs: Egypt's Nubian Rulers*. London: Rubicon Press, 2002.

O'Connor, David. *Ancient Nubia: Egypt's Rival in Africa*. Philadelphia: University of Pennsylvania Museum Publications, 1994.

Service, Pamela F. *The Ancient African Kingdom of Kush*. Tarrytown, NY: Benchmark Books, 1998.

Shinnie, Peter L. *Meroe: A Civilization of the Sudan*. London: Thames and Hudson, 1967.

———. *Ancient Nubia*. London: Kegan Paul, 1996.

Torok, Laszlo. *The City of Meroe: John Garstang's Excavations in the Sudan*. London: Kegan Paul, 1994.

LAW, POLITICS, AND ADMINISTRATION

Kaplan, Leslie C. *Politics and Government in Ancient Egypt*. Primary Sources of Ancient Civilizations: Egypt. New York: Powerkids Press, 2004.

Strudwick, Nigel. *The Administration of Egypt in the Old Kingdom: The Highest Titles and Their Holders*. London, Boston: KPI, 1985.

Versteeg, Russ. *Law in Ancient Egypt*. Durham: Carolina Academic Press, 2002.

MEDICINE AND MAGIC

Breasted, James H. *The Edwin Smith Surgical Papyrus*. Nos. 3 and 4. Chicago: The Oriental Institute, 1991.

Brier, Bob. *Ancient Egyptian Magic*. New York: William Morrow, 1998.

Bryan, Cyril P. *The Papyrus Ebers: Oldest Medical Book in the World*. New York: E C A Associates, 1996.

Ebbell, B. *The Papyrus Ebers: The Greatest Egyptian Medical Document*. Copenhagen: Levin & Munksgaard, 1937.

Estes, J. Worth. *The Medical Skills of Ancient Egypt*. Sagamore Beach, Mass.: Science History Publications, 1993.

Harris, Eleanor L. *Ancient Egyptian Divination and Magic*. York Beach, Maine: Red Wheel/Weiser, 1998.

Manniche, Lise. *An Ancient Egyptian Herbal*. Austin: University of Texas Press, 1989.

Nunn, John F. *Ancient Egyptian Medicine*. Norman: University of Oklahoma Press, 2002.

Pinch, Geraldine. *Magic in Ancient Egypt*. Austin: University of Texas Press, 1995.

MUMMIES AND LIFE AFTER DEATH

Aliki. *Mummies Made in Egypt*. New York: Crowell, 1975.

Aufderheide, Arthur C. *The Scientific Study of Mummies*. Cambridge: Cambridge University Press, 2003.

Brier, Bob. *Egyptian Mummies: Unraveling the Secrets of an Ancient Art*. New York: Quill, 1996.

Faulkner, Raymond O. *The Ancient Egyptian Book of the Dead*. Austin: University of Texas Press, 1990.

Filer, Joyce. *The Mystery of the Egyptian Mummy*. New York: Oxford University Press, 2003.

Goelet, Ogden. *The Egyptian Book of the Dead: The Book of Going Forth by Day*. San Francisco: Chronicle Books, 1994.

Hawass, Zahi A. *Curse of the Pharaohs: My Adventures with Mummies.* Washington, D.C.: National Geographic Society, 2004.

———. *Valley of the Golden Mummies.* New York: Abrams, 2000.

Ikram, Salima. *Death and Burial in Ancient Egypt.* Upper Saddle River, N.J.: Longman, 2003.

Ikram, Salima, and Aidan Dodson. *The Mummy in Ancient Egypt: Equipping the Dead for Eternity.* New York: Thames & Hudson, 1998.

Osborne, Will. *Mummies & Pyramids.* New York: Random House, 2001.

Putnam, James. *Eyewitness: Mummy.* New York: Knopf, 1993.

Taylor, John H. *Death and the Afterlife.* London: The Trustees of the British Museum, 2001.

Trumble, Kelly. *Cat Mummies.* New York: Clarion Books, 1996.

Tyldesley, Joyce A. *The Mummy: Unwrap the Ancient Secrets of the Mummies' Tombs.* London: Carlton, 1999.

Wisseman, Sarah Underhill. *The Virtual Mummy.* Champaign: University of Illinois Press, 2003.

POETRY, LETTERS, AND LITERATURE

Foster, John L. *Ancient Egyptian Literature: An Anthology.* Austin: University of Texas Press, 1991.

———. *Hymns, Prayers and Songs: An Anthology of Ancient Egyptian Lyric Poetry.* Atlanta: Society of Biblical Literature, 1996.

———. *Love Songs of the New Kingdom.* Austin: University of Texas Press, 1992.

Lichtheim, Miriam. *Ancient Egyptian Literature,* Volume I–III. Berkeley: University of California Press, 1975.

Moran, William L. *The Amarna Letters.* Baltimore: Johns Hopkins University Press, 2002.

Parkinson, Richard B. *The Tale of Sinuhe and Other Ancient Egyptian Poems, 1940–1640 BC.* Oxford: Oxford University Press, 1999.

———. *Voices from Ancient Egypt: An Anthology of Middle Kingdom Writings.* Norman: University of Oklahoma Press, 1991.

Simpson, William Kelly, ed. *The Literature of Ancient Egypt: An Anthology of Stories, Instructions, Stelae, Autobiographies, and Poetry,* 3rd ed. New Haven, Conn.: Yale University Press, 2003.

Winters, Kay. *Voices of Ancient Egypt.* Washington, D.C.: National Geographic Society, 2003.

PYRAMIDS AND SPHINX

Hawass, Zahi A. *The Secrets of the Sphinx: Restoration Past and Present.* Cairo: American University in Cairo Press, 1998.

Isler, Martin. *Sticks, Stones, & Shadows: Building the Egyptian Pyramids.* Norman: University of Oklahoma Press, 2001.

Lehner, Mark. *The Complete Pyramids.* London: Thames and Hudson, 1997.

Macaulay, David. *Pyramid.* Boston: Houghton Mifflin, 1982.

Putnam, James. *Eyewitness: Pyramid.* New York: DK Publishing, 2000.

Zivie-Coche, Christiane. *Sphinx: History of a Monument,* trans. David Lorton. Ithaca, N.Y.: Cornell University Press, 2002.

RELIGION/GODS AND GODDESSES

Fisher, Leonard Everett. *The Gods and Goddesses of Ancient Egypt.* New York: Holiday House, 1997.

Lesko, Barbara S. *The Great Goddesses of Egypt.* Norman: University of Oklahoma Press, 1999.

Shafer, Byron E. *Religion in Ancient Egypt: Gods, Myths, and Personal Practice.* Ithaca, N.Y.: Cornell University Press, 1991.

Wilkinson, Richard H. *The Complete Gods and Goddesses of Ancient Egypt.* London: Thames and Hudson, 2003.

VALLEY OF THE KINGS

Berger, Melvin. *Mummies of the Pharaohs: Exploring the Valley of Kings.* Washington, D.C.: National Geographic Society, 2001.

Hornung, Erik. *The Valley of the Kings: Horizon of Eternity,* trans. David Warburton. New York: Timken Publishers, 1990.

Reeves, Nicholas, and Richard H. Wilkinson. *The Complete Valley of the Kings: Tombs and Treasures of Egypt's Greatest Pharaohs.* London: Thames and Hudson, 1996.

Romer, John. *Valley of the Kings: Exploring the Tombs of the Pharaohs.* New York: Henry Holt, 1981.

Smith, Stuart Tyson, and Nancy Stone Bernard. *Valley of the Kings.* New York: Oxford University Press, 2003.

WARFARE

Cottrell, Leonard. *The Warrior Pharaohs.* New York: Putnam, 1969.

Healy, Mark. *Armies of the Pharaohs: New Kingdom Egypt.* London: Osprey, 2000.

Millard, Anne, and Mark Bergin. *Going to War in Ancient Egypt.* London: Franklin Watts, 2000.

Sandars, Nancy K. *The Sea Peoples: Warriors of the Ancient Mediterranean 1250–1150 BC.* Rev. ed. London: Thames and Hudson, 1985.

WOMEN

Hawass, Zahi A. *Silent Images: Women in Pharaonic Egypt.* New York: Abrams, 2000.

Pomeroy, Sarah B. *Goddesses, Whores, Wives, and Slaves: Women in Classical Antiquity.* New York: Schocken, 1995.

Robins, Gay. *Women in Ancient Egypt.* London: British Museum Press, 1993.

Rowlandson, Jane. *Women and Society in Greek and Roman Egypt: A Sourcebook.* Cambridge: Cambridge University Press, 1998.

WEBSITES

GATEWAYS

Tour Egypt
www.touregypt.net/
Provides links to Egyptian Antiquities, Egypt for Kids, Egyptian Recipes, Travel Guide, and more.

Egyptology Resources
www.newton.cam.ac.uk/egypt/
Offers answers to basic questions about Egyptology and features information about ancient and modern Egypt, with links to numerous websites.

Guardian's Ancient Egypt Kid Connection
www.guardians.net/egypt/kids/
A website with Egypt links especially for kids. Includes instructions for building your own model of the Great Pyramid, an introduction to some famous women of ancient Egypt, featuring Nefertiti, Hatshepsut, Cleopatra, Kiya, Tiya, and Nefertari, and a project to make a model of a mummy case with a wrapped mummy inside.

History for Kids
www.historyforkids.org/learn/egypt/index.htm
Learn more about ancient Egypt, including history (with timeline), environment, religion, clothing, food, economy, people, writing (hieroglyphs), games, art, architecture (pyramids), as well as crafts and projects about Egypt.

An Introduction to Pharaonic Egypt
nefertiti.iwebland.com/
Contains information about the history and dynasties of Pharaonic Egypt, as well as sections on mythology, life in ancient Egypt, a bibliography, and links to relevant websites.

WEBSITES

The Ancient Egypt Site
www.ancient-egypt.org/index.html
Allows web visitors to explore more than 3,000 years of ancient Egyptian history, examine the sites and monuments, learn the language and the writing, and link to other sites using the "Hitchhiker's guide to Ancient Egypt."

Ancient Egypt Webquest
www.iwebquest.com/egypt/ancientegypt.htm
Features adventure game for elementary and middle schoolers and information about ancient Egyptian daily life, mummies, hieroglyphics, King Tut (Tutankhamen), games, and archeology.

BBC Egypt Site
www.bbc.co.uk/history/ancient/egyptians/
Website maintained by the BBC contains links to a timeline, games, and essays about a range of topics, including Pharaohs such as Hatshepsut and Ramesses II, pyramids, hieroglyphs, mummies, and women.

British Museum
www.ancientegypt.co.uk/menu.html
The British Museum website for ancient Egypt; includes pages on daily life, geography, gods and goddesses, mummies, pharaohs, pyramids, temples, and writing.

Cairo Museum
www.egyptianmuseum.gov.eg/
Official website of the Cairo Museum in Egypt, with links to breaking news, exhibits, gods, and games.

Digital Egypt
www.digitalegypt.ucl.ac.uk//Welcome.html
Website of the Petrie Museum at University College London. Offers support for teachers and students from different disciplines and includes hundreds of web pages on archaeology, architec-

ture, art, medicine, science, religion, literature, gender studies, cultural studies, and museum studies.

Explore Ancient Egypt

www.mfa.org/egypt/explore_ancient_egypt
Website of the Egyptian Collection at the Boston Museum of Fine Arts, where visitors can learn about archaeology, daily life, hieroglyphs, mummies, and Egyptian style.

Egyptology Online

www.egyptologyonline.com/
Provides information about life in Egypt, chronology, history, pharaohs, monuments, the pyramids, hieroglyphs, Egyptologists, great discoveries, gods and goddesses and religion, and further reading.

The Louvre

www.louvre.fr/anglais/collec/ae/ae_f.htm
The Egyptian Collection at the Louvre museum in Paris includes in-depth discussions on selected pieces, how the collection was formed, a map of ancient Egypt, and a searchable database of the works of art on exhibit at the museum.

Pyramids: The Inside Story

www.pbs.org/wgbh/nova/pyramid/
The website maintained by PBS and Nova contains fun and fascinating material on the pyramids of Giza, the work of Egyptologist Mark Lehner, and an interview with the director of the pyramids, Dr. Zahi Hawass.

Theban Mapping Project

www.thebanmappingproject.com
Site maintained by the Theban Mapping Project (TMP, now based at the American University in Cairo), with information about the Valley of the Kings, including an atlas, articles, timelines, clickable links to specific tombs in the Valley (including King Tut's, no. 62).

Tutankhamun: Anatomy of an Excavation

www.ashmol.ox.ac.uk/gri/4tut.html
The website of the Griffith Institute at Oxford University in England presents the complete records of Howard Carter's excavation of the tomb of Tutankhamun, including a searchable database of all 5,398 finds and Harry Burton's photographs of the tomb and its excavation.

Virtual Egypt

www.virtual-egypt.com
Fun website with lots to do and to download, including screensavers, videos, virtual tours, and a hieroglyph translator.

Virtual Kahun

www.kahun.man.ac.uk
A joint project between the Manchester Museum and the Petrie Museum of Egyptian Archaeology in England, which includes a virtual reality program exploring the houses of ancient Kahun, as well as a gallery of images and information about both the excavations and the collections of objects.

Women in the Ancient World

www.womenintheancientworld.com/index.htm
Contains material on the status, role and daily life of women in the ancient civilizations of Egypt, Rome, Greece, Israel, and Babylonia. The Egypt page provides additional links to topics such as clothing and fashion, economy, Greek and Roman Egypt, health, literacy, royal women, and women and religion.

INDEX

TEXT CREDITS

MAIN TEXT

p. 15: Oliver J. Thatcher, ed. *The Library of Original Sources,* Vol. I: The Ancient World. Milwaukee, Wis.: University Research Extension Co., 1907, 79–83.

p. 17: Thatcher, ed. *The Library of Original Sources,*, 79–83.

p. 19: James Henry Breasted, *Ancient Records of Egypt,* Part I. Champaign: University of Illinois Press, 2001, 160–61.

p. 20: Breasted, *Ancient Records of Egypt,* 160–61.

p. 31: Rosalie and Charles Baker III, *Ancient Egyptians.* New York: Oxford University Press, 2001, 19.

p. 33: James Henry Breasted. *The Edwin Smith Surgical Papyrus.* Oriental Institute Publications, nos. 3, 4. Chicago: The Oriental Institute, 1930, 78, 96.

p. 37: Miriam Lichtheim, *Ancient Egyptian Literature,* Vol. I. Berkeley: University of California Press, 1975, 185.

p. 38: Breasted, *Ancient Records of Egypt,* 217.

p. 43: Breasted, *Ancient Records of Egypt,* 332–37.

p. 44: Frank C. Babbitt, trans., *Plutarch's Moralia.* Cambridge, Mass.: Harvard University Press, 1936, 35–37.

p. 45: Babbitt, trans., *Plutarch's Moralia,* 37.

p. 45: Raymond Faulkner, trans., *The Ancient Egyptian Pyramid Texts.* London: Clarendon Press, 1969, 113–14, 139, 157, 250.

p. 52: Robert K. Ritner, trans., "The Negative Confession," in Simpson, ed. *The Literature of Ancient Egypt,* 275–76.

p. 52: Raymond Faulkner, trans., *The Egyptian Book of the Dead: The Book of Going Forth by Day,* London: Trustees of the British Museum, 1985, 62, 133, 135–37.

p. 53: Faulkner, trans., *The Egyptian Book of the Dead,* 32.

p. 55: Herodotus, *Histories.* Trans. by George Rawlinson. New York: Modern Library, 1942, 156.

p. 61: Faulkner, trans., *The Ancient Egyptian Pyramid Texts,* 163, 183, 257.

p.63: Breasted, *Ancient Records of Egypt,* 320–24.

p. 64: Lichtheim, *Ancient Egyptian Literature,* 151.

p. 64–65: Lichtheim, *Ancient Egyptian Literature,*, 85–86.

p. 66: Herodotus, *Histories,* 163.

p. 66–67: Lichtheim, *Ancient Egyptian Literature,* 166–67.

p. 69: William Kelly Simpson, trans., "The Tale of Sinuhe," in *The Literature of Ancient Egypt,* William Kelly Simpson, ed. 54–66.

p. 70: Homer, *Odyssey.* Trans. by Robert Fagles. New York: Viking, 1996, 131.

p. 71: Diodorus Siculus, *Biblioteca Historica.* Trans. by Edwin Murphy. London: McFarland, 1985, 281.

Cyril P. Bryan, trans., *The Papyrus Ebers.* New York: Appleton, 1931, 53, 91.

Diodorus Siculus, *Biblioteca Historica.*

Herodotus, *Histories,* 155.

p. 73: Bryan, trans., *The Papyrus Ebers,* 80–81, 139.

p. 74: Breasted, *The Edwin Smith Surgical Papyrus,* 104.

p. 76: Manetho, *Aegyptiaca.* Trans. by W. G. Waddell. London: W. Heinemann, 1940, 81–83.

p. 77: Edward F. Wente, "The Quarrel of Apophis and Seqenenre," in Simpson, ed., *The Literature of Ancient Egypt,* pp. 77–80.

p. 80: Josephus, *The Life Against Apion.* Trans. by H. St. J. Thackeray. London: William Heinemann, 1926, 197–99.

p. 82: Breasted, *Ancient Records of Egypt,* Part II, 48, 142–43.

p. 83: Joyce A. Tyldesley, *Daughters of Isis: Women of Ancient Egypt.* New York: Viking, 222.

p. 84: Tyldesley, *Daughters of Isis,* 226.

p. 85: Peter A Clayton, *Chronicle of the Pharaohs: The Reign-By-Reign Record of the Rulers and Dynasties of Ancient Egypt.* London: Thames and Hudson, 1994, 109.

p. 87: Eric H. Cline, *The Battles of Armageddon*. Ann Arbor: University of Michigan Press, 18.

p. 90: William Kelly Simpson, "The Love Songs and the Song of the Harper," in *The Literature of Ancient Egypt*, 308.

p. 91: Bryan, trans., *The Papyrus Ebers*, 153.

p. 92: B. Ebbell, *The Papyrus Ebers*. London: Oxford University Press, 1937, 101.

Rosalind M. and Jacques J. Janssen, *Getting Old in Ancient Egypt*. London: Rubicon Press, 1996, 96–97.

p. 93: Bryan, trans., *The Papyrus Ebers*,, 156–157.

p. 94: William Kelly Simpson, trans., "The Shipwrecked Sailor." In *The Literature of Ancient Egypt*, 45–53.

Vincent A. Tobin, trans., "The Tale of the Eloquent Peasant." In *The Literature of Ancient Egypt*, 3rd ed. William Kelly Simpson, ed., 25–44.

Lichtheim, *Ancient Egyptian Literature*, Vol. II, 192–193.

Herodotus, *Histories*. Trans. by George Rawlinson. New York: Modern Library, 1942, 155; quoted in Pierre Montet, *Everyday Life in Egypt in the Days of Ramesses the Great*, Philadelphia: University of Pennsylvania Press, 57.

p. 96: Breasted, *Ancient Records of Egypt*, Part II, 344–45.

Breasted, *Ancient Records of Egypt*, Part II, 345–46.

p. 97: Breasted, *Ancient Records of Egypt*, Part II, 348–49.

Breasted, *Ancient Records of Egypt*, Part I, 202.

Nina M Davies and Sir Alan H. Gardiner, *The tomb of Amenemhet (no. 82)*. London: Egypt Exploration Fund, 1915.

p. 100: Diodorus Siculus, *Histories*, 263–65.

p. 103: William L. Moran, *The Amarna Letters*. Baltimore, Md.: John Hopkins Press, 2002, 61.

p. 104: Moran, *The Amarna Letters*, 292–93.

p. 105: Moran, *The Amarna Letters*, 8–9.

Moran, *The Amarna Letters*, 114–15.

p. 106: Moran, *The Amarna Letters*, 84–86.

Moran, *The Amarna Letters*, 130–31.

p. 108: Lichtheim, *Ancient Egyptian Literature*, Vol. I, 70.

p. 109: Moran, *The Amarna Letters*, 43–46.

p. 110: Homer, *Iliad*. Robert Fagles, trans. New York: Penguin, 1991, 264.

p. 112: Simpson, trans., *The Literature of Ancient Egypt*, 283.

p. 113: Simpson, trans., *The Literature of Ancient Egypt*, 280–281.

p. 114: Simpson, trans., *The Literature of Ancient Egypt*, 283.

Moran, *The Amarna Letters*., 142–48.

p. 115: *Tutankhamun: Anatomy of an Excavation*, Howard Carter's diaries. Updated and republished at: *www.ashmol.ox.ac.uk/gri/4sea1no2.html*.

p. 116: *Tutankhamun: Anatomy of an Excavation*.

p. 117: *Tutankhamun: Anatomy of an Excavation*.

p. 118: *Tutankhamun: Anatomy of an Excavation*.

p. 122: Strabo, *Geography*. Horace Leonard Jones, trans. London: W. Heinemann, 1917, 153.

p. 123: John F. Nunn, *Ancient Egyptian Medicine*, Norman: University of Oklahoma Press, 1996, 191–192.

Marie Parsons, "Childbirth and Children in Ancient Egypt." *www.touregypt.net/featurestories/mothers.htm*.

Bryan, trans., *The Papyrus Ebers*.Quoted in Montet, *Everyday Life in Egypt in the Days of Ramesses the Great*, 58.

p. 124: Marie Parsons, "Childbirth and Children in Ancient Egypt."

p. 126: Marie Parsons, "Childbirth and Children in Ancient Egypt."

p. 127: William Kelly Simpson, "The Scribal Traditions in the Schools," in Simpson, ed., *The Literature of Ancient Egypt*.

Lichtheim, *Ancient Egyptian Literature,* Vol. II, 136.

Simpson, ed., *The Literature of Ancient Egypt*, 307.

p. 128: Breasted, *Ancient Records of Egypt,* Part III, 136–57.

p. 130: Breasted, *Ancient Records of Egypt,* 136–57.

p. 131: Breasted, *Ancient Records of Egypt,* 136–57.

p. 132: Breasted, *Ancient Records of Egypt,* 136–57.

p. 134: Breasted, *Ancient Records of Egypt,* 136–57.

Breasted, *Ancient Records of Egypt,,* 165–74.

p. 136: Bryan, trans., *The Papyrus Ebers,* 163–66.

p. 137: Andrea G. McDowell, *Village Life in Ancient Egypt: Laundry Lists and Love Songs.* New York: Oxford University Press, 2002, 66.

p. 138: Tyldesley, *Daughters of Isis,* 86.

p. 140: McDowell, *Village Life in Ancient Egypt*, 29.

p. 141: Breasted, *Ancient Records of Egypt,* 33–49.

p. 142: Breasted, *Ancient Records of Egypt,* 33–49.

p. 143: Breasted, *Ancient Records of Egypt,* 33–49.

p. 144: Breasted, *Ancient Records of Egypt,* 33–49.

p. 147: Aldokken, *www.aldokkan.com/art/cinderella.htm.*

p. 148: Aldokken.

p. 149: Aldokken.

p. 151: "The Report of Wenamun," Edward F. Wente, trans. In Simpson, ed., *The Literature of Ancient Egypt,* 3rd ed., 116–24.

p. 153: Breasted, *Ancient Records of Egypt,* 418–44.

p. 155: Breasted, *Ancient Records of Egypt,* 418–44.

p. 156: Breasted, *Ancient Records of Egypt,* 418–44.

p. 157: John Langhorne and William Langhorne, eds., *Plutarch's Lives, Translated from the Original Greek.* Cincinnati, Ohio: Applegate, Pounsford and Co., 1874, 434–39.

p. 158: Langhorne and Langhorne, eds., *Plutarch's Lives,* 434–439.

p. 161: Langhorne and Langhorne, eds., *Plutarch's Lives,* 434–439.

Homer, *Odyssey,* Trans. by Robert Fagles. New York: Penguin, 1999, 354–55.

Arrian, *The Campaigns of Alexander,* Aubrey De Selincourt, trans. New York: Penguin, 1981.

p. 162: Langhorne and Langhorne, eds., *Plutarch's Lives,* 434–39.

p. 163: Langhorne and Langhorne, eds., *Plutarch's Lives,* 434–39.

p. 164: Edith Flamarion, *Cleopatra: Life and Death of a Pharaoh.* New York: Harry N. Abrams, Inc., 1997, 20.

p. 166: Peter Clayton, *The Seven Wonders of the Ancient World.* London: Routledge, 1988, 146.

Peter Clayton, *The Seven Wonders of the Ancient World.* London: Routledge, 1988, 143.

p. 167: Plutarch, *Life of Antony,* 27.2–3. In Plutarch, *Makers of Rome.* New York: Penguin, 1965, 294.

p. 169: Charles Knight, ed. *The Works of William Shakspere.* London: Routledge, 1875, 413–414.

p. 170–71: C. G. Kühn, *Galeni Opera Omnia,* vol. II. Leipzig: C. Cnobloch, 1821–1833. Reprint, L. Edelstein, trans., 1965, 220.

p. 172: Hero of Alexandria, *Dictionary of Scientific Biography.* New York: Scribner, 1972, 314–15.

Liba C. Taub, *Ptolemy's Universe.* Chicago, Ill.: Open Court, 1993, vii.

SIDEBARS

p. 40: Lichtheim, *Ancient Egyptian Literature* Vol. II, 168–70.

p. 123: Naphtali Lewis, *Life in Egypt Under Roman Rule,* Oxford: Clarendon Press, 1985, 54.